BULLEID AND THE TURF BURNER

AND OTHER EXPERIMENTS WITH IRISH STEAM TRACTION

BULLEID AND THE TURF BURNER

AND OTHER EXPERIMENTS WITH IRISH STEAM TRACTION

Ernie Shepherd

KRB Publications

KRB Publications
PO Box 269
SOUTHAMPTON
SO30 4XR

www.krbpublications.co.uk

ISBN 0954203585

Printed by the Amadeus Press

CONTENTS

Front Cover: Main view: CC1 on early trails.   (CIE)
                Colour view, top: CC1 at Inchicore when brand new.
                Colour view, bottom: Forlorn and forgotten. CC1 awaiting the cutter's torch.   (both Colour Rail)

Title Page: CC1 unnumbered and in workshop grey on load-starting trials at Inchicore Works on 15th August 1957. The
                load was shown as 330 tons, equal to 22 six-wheelers. Some lineside fires were started due to the ejection of
                burning turf particles.   (CIE)

This Page: O.V. Bulleid and his children with his parents-in-law, H.A. Ivatt and Mrs Ivatt, photographed by his wife
                in 1920.   (M.C. Bulleid)

INTRODUCTION and ACKNOWLEDGEMENTS

The period beginning with the outbreak of war in 1939 and ending with the demise of steam in the 1960s was a difficult one for the railways in the Republic of Ireland, in particular, Córas Iompair Éireann, due to shortages of fuel, a severe backlog of maintenance and replacement, and finally problems associated with the introduction of the Metropolitan Vickers diesel locomotives. Whilst this narrative is intended as an update to Peter Rowledge's book on the turf-burning prototype locomotive, it was felt that some background information on these wartime difficulties would set the scene. Additional material has come to light in recent times, including a file of papers containing a lengthy and detailed report prepared for O.V.S. Bulleid by the late John Click shortly after the completion of road trials of CC1 in October 1957. Subsequently, further official papers came to light which not only dealt with the turf-burning experiments, but also made reference to other items of interest which were considered or occurred during the late 1940s and the 1950s. The story of the Metrovicks has been told in the Journals of the Irish Railway Record Society and will not therefore be repeated here.

It would not have been possible to have written this story without assistance from a number of sources. Early on in the author's researches, the name of Séan Heneghan was mentioned by a number of people as somebody to contact. Séan had been appointed Technical Assistant to oversee the tests with the experimental turf-burning locomotive No 356 and he was able to add a good deal to our knowledge of those tests and the associated difficulties encountered. Tony Jackson was in the office of the Chief Chemist and Metallurgist at Inchicore at the time when CC1 was being built and, whilst he had no direct involvement with the Turf Burner, he nevertheless has been able to add some useful comments. A chance letter to Messrs. Ricardo Consulting Engineers of Shoreham-by-Sea in West Sussex proved to be of immense assistance. This firm had acted as consulting engineers to CIE for a period of eighteen months during a critical period in the design stage of the prototype locomotive. They very generously provided the author with a photocopy of their complete file of correspondence with Bulleid. These papers added considerably to our knowledge of Bulleid's ideas, some of which were completely unknown to the author; it is only a pity that Bulleid's own correspondence files are unavailable. Peter Rowledge was only too happy to allow the present author to use whatever he wished from his publication.

The excellent drawings are the work of Alan Roome. Alan had originally produced these drawings for Peter Rowledge's book on the Turf Burner published by the London Area of the Irish Railway Record Society in 1972. The originals came from CIE in Inchicore, via the IRRS Archives in Dublin, in whose care they have been entrusted. I am grateful to Joseph Leckey, Honorary Archivist of the IRRS, for the use of these, and to the Assistant Archivist, Brendan Pender, for his assistance in turning out this material. Kevin Robertson, author of *Leader, Steam's Last Chance,* gave his moral support and permission to use extracts from his book. Grateful thanks are also due to KRB Publications for their faith in agreeing to publish the manuscript. Gerry Beesley provided the information in regard to the peat-fired generating stations belonging to the Electricity Supply Board. To all of these people the author is extremely grateful. If anybody else has been left out, it was entirely unintentional and they are requested to accept this general thank you and apology for the omission. Similarly, all photographs are credited where the photographer is known.

Apart from the official correspondence files already referred to, the Board Minute books of various pre-grouping companies provided material on turf-burning experiments during the 19th century. A number of other sources have been used in the author's researches, including the following:

A Lifetime with Locomotives: Bond, Roland C.; Goose & Son, Cambridge 1975.
Bulleid, Last Giant of Steam: Day-Lewis, Séan; George Allen & Unwin, London 1964.
Bulleid Power, the 'Merchant Navy' Class: Fry, A.J.; Alan Sutton Publishing Ltd, Stroud, 1996
Bulleid, the Designer who Dared to be Different: Click, J.G.; Steam World, Oct. & Nov. 1982.
GNR(I) Working Timetables, various.
GSR Working Timetables, various.
Irish Railfans' News.
Irish Railways since 1916: Baker, Michael H.C.; Ian Allan, London 1972.
Irish Steam Locomotive Register: Rowledge, J.W.P.; Irish Traction Group, Stockport 1993.
Journals of the Irish Railway Record Society.
Leader, Steam's Last Chance: Robertson, Kevin; Alan Sutton Publishing Ltd., Gloucester 1988.
Locomotive Engineers' Pocketbook: The Locomotive Publishing Co Ltd, London.
Oil-burning Locomotives – General Instructions: Córas Iompair Éireann, Dublin (undated).
On the Move - Córas Iompair Éireann 1945-95: O Riain, M.; Gill & Macmillan, Dublin 1995.
Railway Fuel Problems: Dudley, J.H. – a paper presented to the Irish Railway Record Society.
Reports of Tribunal on Public Transport: Leydon, J.; Stationery Office, Dublin, 1939.
Report on Transport in Ireland: Milne, Sir James; Stationery Office, Dublin, 1948.
Report of Committee of Inquiry into Internal Transport: Beddy, J.P.; Stationery Office, Dublin, 1957.
The Schull & Skibbereen Railway: Boyd, James I.C.; The Oakwood Press, Usk 1999.
The Turfburner, Ireland's last Steam Locomotive Design: Rowledge, J.W.P.; IRRS London Area 1972.
Twentieth Century Irish Locomotives: Shepherd, W.E.; Union Publications, London 1966.

BULLEID AND THE TURF BURNER

For those technically minded readers, typical relative calorific values for coal, turf and oil are as follows:

	Calorific value per lb	BTUs per lb
Welsh coal	8,402	15,123
Turf (30% water)	3,000	5,400
Turf (10% water)	5,000	9,000
American oil	10,904	19,627
Russian oil	10,800	19,440

Abbreviations Used

B&NCR	Belfast & Northern Counties Railway
BnM	Bórd na Móna
BR	British Railways
BRCW	Birmingham Railway Carriage & Wagon Co Ltd
CIE	Córas Iompair Éireann
CME	Chief Mechanical Engineer
D&SE	Dublin & South Eastern (section of CIE)
ESB	Electricity Supply Board
GM	General Motors Corporation (Electro-Motive Division)
GNR	Great Northern Railway (England)
GNR(I)	Great Northern Railway (Ireland)
GS&WR	Great Southern & Western Railway
GSR	Great Southern Railways
L&NER	London & North Eastern Railway
MGWR	Midland Great Western Railway
SR	Southern Railway (England)
TDB	Turf Development Board
W&LR	Waterford & Limerick Railway

SOME OF THE PERSONALITIES INVOLVED

Listed below are brief biographical details of some of the personalities involved in the events described in this book. Some further details will be found in the text, including those on O.V.S. Bulleid himself.

Dr. Christopher Stephen Andrews
Dr C.S. (Todd) Andrews was born in Dublin on 6th October 1901, and was a commercial graduate of University College Dublin. As an official of the Department for Industry & Commerce in 1933, Andrews was given responsibility for the commercial development of turf in Ireland. The initial emphasis was on the production and marketing of hand-won turf. The Turf Development Board was set up in 1934 as an autonomous body. Later, the Turf Development Act of 1946 set up Bórd na Móna, Andrews being appointed Chairman of that company in 1958.

With the progress of building turf-burning power stations nearing completion, Andrews was offered the post of full-time chairman of CIE in 1958. He took up office on 1st September 1958, initially for a five year period. It was not long before CIE suffered the severest shake-up in its history up to that time, when Andrews introduced the concept of area manage-

Group at Inchicore Works. O.V.S. Bulleid (on right with hat and glasses), Frank Lemass - General Manager (on his own in the middle), Thaddeus C. Countney - CIE Chairman (sixth from left), and M.J. Hayes - Company Secretary (third from left). In the background is Bulleid's company car.

(Rex Roberts Studio, copyright CIE)

BULLEID AND THE TURF BURNER

A party of visiting dignitaries and Inchicore staff in front of 960hp Sulzer A1A-A1A No B112 at Inchicore in May 1958. On the extreme left is O.V.S. Bulleid. Some others identified include Lucas Collins (front row with arms folded), Jackie Johnston (front row holding papers), Dick Grainger (middle row to left of Johnston), M.J. Hayes (back row to left of loco number, dark hair and glasses), and Matt Devereux (back row, left hand side immediately below where the light stripe ends on the loco).

(Rex Roberts Studio, copyright CIE)

ment. Later again, he was to become the Dr Beeching of CIE as many unremunerative branch lines were closed down. In addition, Andrews became involved in several staff disputes as he endeavoured to put the transport company on a sound financial footing. Despite this, he remained as Chairman of CIE until 16th September 1966, having in the interim also become Chairman of the national broadcaster, Radio Telefis Eireann. He will perhaps be best remembered for the closure of the Dublin suburban line from Harcourt Street to Shanganagh Junction.

Thekla Beere
Miss Thekla Beere was born in Kells, Co. Meath in 1901, and was described as a civil servant and transport and labour relations expert. The first woman to head a Government department, she became Secretary to the Department for Industry & Commerce.

Edgar Craven Bredin
E.C. Bredin was the son of Col Alexander Bredin of Prospect, Co. Longford. He was educated at Mountjoy School, Dublin, and began his engineering career at Gloucester. Bredin joined the staff of the GS&WR at Inchicore in 1907 in the locomotive engineer's office. He was involved in experiments and research connected with fuel consumption. In due course he became Assistant Works Manager at Inchicore and Works Manager in 1921. Following on the formation of the GSR, he carried out the reorganisation of the locomotive works.

Bredin was appointed Chief Mechanical Engineer in 1937 and was responsible for the design of the massive 800 class 4-6-0 locomotives introduced in 1939. He became Deputy General Manager in 1941 and General Manager on the retirement of his predecessor, W.H. Morton in 1942. Bredin retired from CIE in 1946 after thirty-nine years service, remaining for a time in a consultancy capacity. He died in a private nursing

2

SOME OF THE PERSONALITIES INVOLVED

home on 3rd August 1950, and is buried in Dublin.

Thaddeus Cornelius (Ted) Courtney
T.C. Courtney was a native of Cork, and graduated from University College Cork with a civil engineering degree. His first job was with the Cork Bandon & South Coast Railway but he soon moved on to become involved in the construction of Messrs Ford's motor factory in Cork and Messrs Harland & Wolff in Belfast. Having served in the National Army in 1922, Courtney became involved in local government three years later. He served for a time as County Surveyor for the North Riding of Co. Tipperary, before joining the Department of Local Government in 1934. He became involved in the county council turf production schemes and in the Turf Development Board in 1941, there working closely with C.S. (later Dr) Andrews. Courtney served as Railway Inspecting Officer with the Department for Industry & Commerce from 1939 to 1949.

Courtney became Chairman of CIE in February 1949 on the retirement of A.P. Reynolds. Within a month, he engaged George B. Howden, General Manager and former Chief Mechanical Engineer of the GNR(I) in a consultancy capacity. Howden became General Manager of CIE a year later, Frank Lemass becoming Chief Officer. Courtney announced his resignation as Chairman at a board meeting on 28th August 1958. He was sixty-three years of age and was suffering from ill health. He remained on as a non-executive director.

George B Howden
G.B. Howden was of Scottish parentage, and started his railway career with the North British Railway, later becoming assistant engineer of the Scottish area of the London & North Eastern Railway. In 1929, he accepted the position of Chief Engineer to the GNR(I), becoming in addition Mechanical Engineer four years later. Howden was appointed General Manager of the GNR(I) in 1939. As stated above he was also appointed General Manager of CIE in 1950. He only remained in this post until 1953 when he became General Manager of the Ulster Transport Authority in Belfast. Howden retired in 1963 at the age of seventy-three and died on 22nd January 1966.

J.J. (Jackie) Johnston
Jackie Johnston was apprenticed to the GS&WR at Inchicore in 1920. After serving his time, he transferred to Limerick for some years, and then returned to the Drawing Office at Inchicore. He was involved in the design of the mechanical portion of the Drumm battery experiments and was also closely involved with Bredin in the design work on the 800 class locomotives. Johnston was appointed Assistant Works Manager in 1943 and Chief Draughtsman in 1945. Appointed Assistant Chief Mechanical Engineer in 1949, Johnson retired in 1969.

Frank Lemass
Frank Lemass was the brother of Séan Lemass, Minister for Industry & Commerce between March 1957 and June 1959,

later to become Taoiseach (Prime Minister). Frank was an accountant by profession, and had been with the firm of Messrs Craig Gardner, who were auditors to the old Dublin United Transport Company (DUTC). They later became auditors to CIE. Lemass became Assistant General Manager of CIE on its formation in January 1945, having previously been General Manager of the DUTC. When Edgar Bredin retired as General Manager in 1946, Lemass took over that position and, apart from the period 1950 to 1953 when he was Chief Officer, he remained as General Manager until 1970. Frank Lemass died on 24th June 1974. He had for some years prior to his death been an honorary member of the Irish Railway Record Society.

Cecil F. Tyndall
C.F. Tyndall was educated at Castleknock College, Dublin, and began his training with the GS&WR at Inchicore in 1917, being appointed Assistant to the Works Manager in 1924. On the formation of the GSR a year later, he became Senior Assistant to the Running Superintendent. In 1930 he was appointed Assistant District Locomotive Superintendent for the Cork area and in 1937 took charge of the Waterford district. He became Running Superintendent in June 1942. On the formation of CIE in January 1945, Tyndall undertook, the post of Mechanical Engineer and remained in control of both departments for the next five years. In 1947 his title was altered to Chief Motive Power Engineer. During the later war and post-war years, Tyndall was involved with the introduction of the oil-burning locomotives, as well as the use of pulverised fuel and briquettes. He retired from CIE on 31st December 1952.

Lucas Collins
Although strictly speaking not a player in the story to be unfolded, Lucas Collins was appointed as Bulleid's successor on the latter's retirement in 1958. Collins was born in Dublin in 1917, being educated at Presentation College in Glasthule. He obtained his BE and BSc degrees at University College Dublin (UCD). After spending some years with Messrs British Thomson Houston at Rugby, he returned to UCD as a demonstrator in mechanical engineering. He then joined the Turf Development Board as a Junior Mechanical Engineer in 1942, being appointed Assistant Chief Engineer in June 1944. On the formation of BnM in 1946, he became Chief Mechanical Engineer. He was appointed Mechanical Engineer on Bulleid's departure from Inchicore in 1958, the title 'Chief' being dropped from the job description as all engineering, mechanical and civil was by then under the control of the Chief Engineer, Dan Herlihy. Collins became Assistant General Manager (Engineering) in 1966, at which time Matt Devereux was appointed Chief Mechanical Engineer.

It will be obvious from the foregoing biographies that many of the people involved in the story of the Turf Burner had previously worked together, either in the TDB or with BnM.

Signed photograph of O.V.S. Bulleid and M. Louis Armand of the SNCF in the cab of 'CC1' on 8th August 1957. The locomotive had been in 'collision' with DE No 1100 on the previous day and was hastily repaired for Armand's visit. The original of this photograph was presented to Séan Heneghan by Bulleid. There is no record of any visit to view CC1 by André Chapelon.

(CIE)

EARLY EXPERIMENTS WITH TURF

Turf, or peat as it is perhaps more widely known outside Ireland, consists of accumulations of plant remains that have been prevented from decaying by becoming water-logged. Turf is almost entirely comprised of organic matter and has a low ash content. Turf production in the Twenty-six Counties has been overseen since 1934 by the Turf Development Board, a private company with State financial assistance, and since 1946 by Bórd na Móna (Turf Board), a semi-state body. This latter body has extracted turf from very large tracts of bog using large harvesting machines, annual output being in the order of five million tons.

Peat is frequently referred to in Ireland as turf, although strictly speaking, the two words are not synonymous. The former consists of vegetable matter decomposed by the action of water in bogs etc, and partly carbonised; it can also refer to such material cut in pieces for use as fuel. Turf on the other hand, consists of short grass and the surface layer of earth bound together by its roots; in addition, however, the *Oxford Dictionary* also refers to turf as being a slab of peat

for fuel. The Irish word Móin translates as turf, peat, bogland or a moor, adding further to possible confusion. Bórd na Móna can therefore be taken to mean either the Peat Board or the Turf Board. Bulleid, in correspondence, sometimes referred to peat, sometimes to turf; even BnM used both terms in correspondence. In our narrative we will employ both terms according to the source material.

Turf as a potential fuel suffers from its high moisture content. As an example, approximately ten tons of turf harvested from the bog produces in the region of one ton of dry turf. Machine-won turf is removed by a machine that reaches to the bottom of the turf layer with a chain of bucket cutters. The wet turf is dropped into a macerator which thoroughly mixes and breaks it up. It leaves this machine in a 4in by 4in ribbon and is cut in blocks, which are left to dry in the open. Depending on the weather, moisture content is reduced to about 30%, the calorific value at this stage being about 6,500 BTU. The BnM plant at Lullymore in Co. Kildare produces turf in briquette form, which provides a more compact, very

J15 (101) class 0-6-0 No 121 in more or less original condition at Grand Canal Street, Dublin. Note round-topped, saturated, boiler and unusual McDonnell design of double smokebox door. The fleet of turf-burning locomotives was intended to replace engines such as the J15s.

(H. Fayle, IRRS collection)

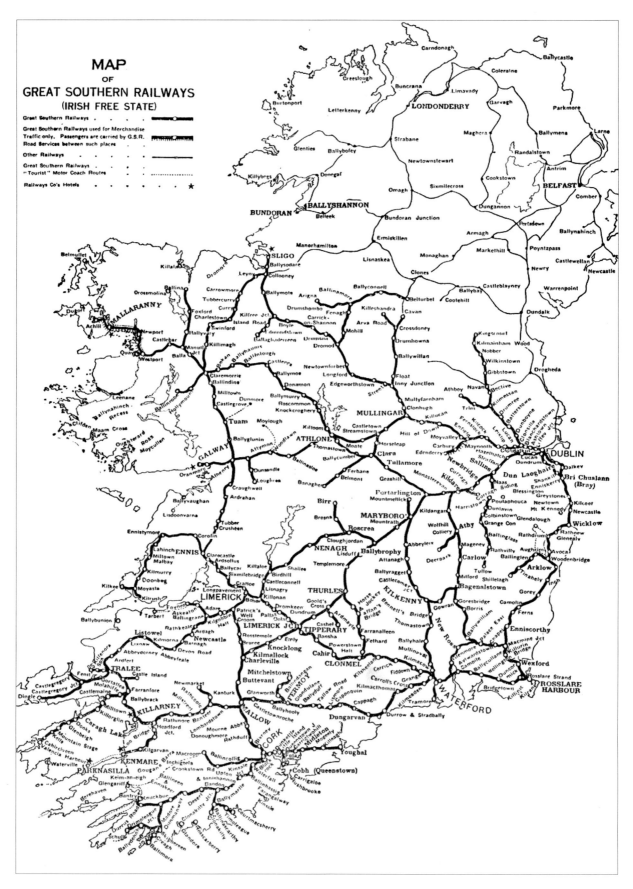

MAP
OF
GREAT SOUTHERN RAILWAYS
(IRISH FREE STATE)

Great Southern Railways	.	.	.	.	.	.	.	━━━◯━━━
Great Southern Railways used for Merchandise Traffic only. Passengers are carried by G.S.R. Road Services between such places	.	.	━━▭━━▭━━
Other Railways	.	.	.	.	.	.	.	━━━━━━
Great Southern Railways "Tourist" Motor Coach Routes	.	.	.	⋯⋯⋯⋯
Railways Co's Hotels	.	.	.	.	.	★

dense, fuel with a moisture content as low as 20% and calorific value of about 7,200BTU. At the time of the trials in the 1950s, turf provided by BnM cost 66s per ton as against 166s for Welsh coal.

The first known reference to the use of turf in a railway locomotive in Ireland was in the Midland Great Western Railway board minutes for 31st August 1848, when the Locomotive Superintendent, John Dewrance, was authorised to obtain a boat load of black turf for "the new engine". This most likely refers to one of the Fairbairn 2-2-2s built in that year. A further reference in November 1848 alludes to Dewrance's proposal to use turf in engines. However, we know that by the following April, authority had been given to erect coke ovens at Broadstone. A newspaper report of October 1849 refers to Waterford & Limerick Railway engines using turf on the Limerick to Tipperary section. There was also a reference to a house being burnt down at Pallisgreen due to 'flakes of fire falling from the engine as it passed by'.

On the Great Southern & Western Railway system, reference was made in April 1855 to the conversion of turf into coke. A Mr. Willans, who had made some improvements in the manufacturing of turf into coke, fit for locomotive purposes, applied for permission to prepare some of this fuel at the (Coke) Ovens at Inchicore that it might be tried in the company's engines. George Miller, the Locomotive Superintendent, was ordered to give Willans whatever assistance he thought proper. In December 1863, a cattle train was inadvertently sent from Inchicore to Kingsbridge on the wrong line. The error resulted from the absence of the pointsman, who, we are told, was engaged at the time in carrying turf to an engine, although this was most likely for lighting-up purposes only. About this time, a Mr. Stokes offered to supply the company with turf delivered at Athy at £3 10s 0d per 100 boxes, he being offered 8d per box, delivered at Kilberry siding, while in November 1865, it was ordered that a siding at 75miles on the mainline be removed, as it was no longer required for the loading of turf.

We do know with some certainty that the Belfast & Northern Counties Railway carried out trials with turf in 1862, but the reported figures are somewhat suspect. One account, which from the details stated would appear to have been a run from Greenisland to Limavady Junction, shows a journey time of 3 hours and 9 minutes, including stops, for the 74 mile run. The train of seven carriages was recorded to weigh 70 tons, including the engine and tender. This latter was possibly either a Sharp 2-4-0 of 1856 or one of the Ballymena, Ballymoney, Coleraine & Portrush Junction Railway 2-2-2s. Total fuel consumption is given as 1,610lb, equating to 21.47lb per mile. This seems to be an impossibly low figure for turf on its own, even allowing for the light weight of the train and the comparatively diminutive engine. Coal consumption in comparison was said to have averaged 26.29lb per mile over a period of one month.

The turf used was described as being of superior quality, and it was also reported that a smaller quantity of turf was required than was necessary of coal. The report from the contemporary press went on to record that the engine produced so much steam that the damper was closed and the firehole door opened for the entire duration of the journey. After the run very little ash and clinker were found and the conclusion was that condensed turf "was in every way well adapted as a fuel for locomotive purposes". Despite these most promising results, there is no evidence that the B&NCR or any other Irish railway used turf other than on an experimental basis.

Reference has already been made to the GS&WR. Following a visit to, and subsequent correspondence with, the Bavarian State Railways, Alexander McDonnell, the Locomotive Superintendent, carried out experiments with turf in 1872. A goods engine ran a distance of 347 miles on light goods work with a consumption of 73.9lb per mile of turf, similar runs with a slightly heavier train showing a consumption of 36.1lb of Welsh coal. With a train of similar weight to the turf experiment, this latter figure might have been reduced to 32-33lb per mile. These tests were presumably carried out with a 101 class 0-6-0 locomotive. Similar tests were carried out with passenger trains. One engine ran for 320 miles with a maximum load of fourteen carriages, achieving a figure of 51.6lb per mile with turf; average speed was 29 miles per hour. The same (unidentified) engine ran a total of 663 miles with an average load of 6.4 carriages, averaging 30 mph and using 20.3lb of coal per mile. A third trial over 694 miles with a similar load and speed recorded 48.9lb per mile with turf and 22-23lb with coal. The tests indicated 100 tons of turf equating to between 43 and 47 tons of coal.

In February 1873, the Works Committee minutes refer to a drawing submitted by McDonnell of a peat making machine which Messrs Courtney & Stephens of Dublin designed for him, along with plans of a "rough inexpensive shed, both for the purpose of making a trial of the utilisation of peat fuel on this line". He was authorised to spend a sum not exceeding £300. Further entries during 1874 and 1875 make reference to purchase of peat for delivery on the Canal Bank at Inchicore, and interestingly to a Mr. Meadows and other gentlemen being allowed "the use of the Company's Peat Works at Mountrath". McDonnell was to be supplied with some of the turf, but later in February 1878, the company would not bind themselves to use any of the turf fuel although disposed to make a trial of it. This would appear to indicate that experiments with the use of this fuel may have continued on and off for some years. A brief reference is also made to the Listowel & Ballybunion Railway using turf in 1917, showing an apparent saving of 10% in fuel costs. There are no further details of this latter experiment, nor of the short-term use of turf on the Schull & Skibbereen narrow-gauge line in West Cork during the Second World War.

Great Southern Railways 700 class 0-6-0 No 704 with the tender enlarged with a creal to carry turf during the Emergency.

(CIE)

GNR(I) S class 4-4-0 No 173 "Galteemore". A very similar locomotive, S2 class No 190 "Lugnaquilla" (named after a mountain in Co. Wicklow) underwent trials burning turf in July 1941.

(H. Fayle, IRRS collection)

FUEL PROBLEMS DURING THE 1940s

Before proceeding to outline later turf-burning developments, it would be useful to take a brief look at the situation that pertained just before the outbreak of World War Two. For a period of approximately 100 years up to the beginning of 1940, Britain and Ireland had ready access to the best of steam coals at affordable prices. Because of this, steam locomotive design in these islands was primarily based on the use of such coal. In 1939, the Great Southern Railways had just over 500 such locomotives in traffic, admittedly, as we shall see a little later, with little standardisation.

There are three principal criteria for the use of coal in locomotive boilers:

[1] The volatile (or gas) content. This was a vital figure on which depended ease of lighting and, perhaps more importantly, the capacity for a locomotive to respond to sudden demands for additional power. It had a sharply defined maximum because even a few percent above the desirable maximum produced excessive consumption.

[2] Fixed carbon. The proportion of coal not convertible into gas, the solid matter that burns as coke and is known by enginemen as the 'firebed'.

[3] Ash content. Non-combustible matter. Ash of low melting point is the basis of clinker, which has over the years defeated many struggling enginemen. Clinker was described by one engineer as being like a serious disease; once it commenced, it spread rapidly, resulting in engine failures unless operated upon.

The first problems began to emerge in late 1940 due to the almost non-availability of imported coal. The GSR found itself using anthracite dust, or "duff". It was very fine – most of it could be passed through an $1/8$ in screen – and because of its fine nature it precluded air passage and it fell through the firebars. The volatile content was in the region of 8% so the burning rate was low. Initially it was added mainly to a stabilised fire made up of what small quantities of good Welsh coal were available. As stocks of the latter dwindled, experiments were made with timber in an attempt to raise the volatile content and retain the air spaces, only freshly cut native timber being available. Briquetting the duff using pitch as a bonding agent to increase the volatile content was tried, but this proved counter-productive as the pitch content fouled up the tubes.

Various other mixtures were added to the anthracite dust and experimented with, notably weak cement, sawdust and cement, and turf mould and cement. All of these experiments, which continued through 1941, failed. Either the cement bond cracked within a short time of being exposed to the fire or the volatile matter burnt away, causing the briquette to collapse. By the end of that year the service was rapidly approaching a state of chaos. At one point only three days coal supplies remained despite the severe cuts in services. The Government stepped in and made available some stocks of coal, but for which the railway would inevitably have closed down entirely.

It is clear that thoughts had by this time turned to the possible use of turf. In September 1941, W.H. Morton, the General Manager, wrote to the Chief Mechanical Engineer, E. C. Bredin, suggesting that substantial stocks of turf be built up at stations for future use, "including in locomotives, if necessary". In October, Bredin, who had now been appointed General Manager following Morton's retirement, wrote to M. J. Ginnety, Chief Mechanical Engineer, at Inchicore again on the same subject, while in December the Stores Superintendent, J.P. Meadows, was pursuing the matter of turf supplies for use on the branches from Mallow to Newmarket and Mitchelstown. Early in January 1942, Meadows reported that 1,702 tons of turf had been used in locomotives up to the end of the year 1941.

The service was again on the brink of collapse in March 1942, goods train journeys that were scheduled to take up to five hours taking anything up to three days to complete. Trains, both goods and passenger, were stranded all over the country, many of the failures resulting from the build-up of clinker, necessitating fire dropping. Lorries were often sent out with timber and hand-picked coal to rescue engines stranded at wayside stations. The clinker, which was the cause of almost all of these failures, used to merge with the firebars, fusing them into a solid mass. On such occasions, engines often had to be abandoned, a procedure known as "baling out". The foreman of a mainline depot sent his superintendent a telegram stating simply, "Driver baled out here at 3 a.m." This was to lead within hours to an investigation of the circumstances by the Garda detective branch! It was about this time that a circular was issued from the General Manager's office exhorting staff to be extra vigilant in regard to the possibility of German troops endeavouring to capture railway installations and the like. Clear instructions were given that signal cabins etc were to be locked on the approach of such troops. These failures had another effect, namely the reduction of the effective number of wagons available for traffic.

Loads of trains were reduced by between 15% and 25% in August 1942 in an attempt to improve timekeeping. At the same time, organised fire-cleaning was introduced and additional time allowed at certain stations, mainly where there were locomotive depots, for that purpose. Some additional locations were included, for example Sallins, where trains arrived following the gruelling climb all the way from Kingsbridge. These measures had the effect of reducing the number of failures in section, which was vital because these failures had a back-up effect, trains sometimes being stopped up to forty miles behind such a failure. These trains in turn ran into problems with fires dying down due to lack of draught. One failure in section could therefore have a serious knock-on effect. Timetables were altered accordingly, and this was to last even post-war. Appendix C indicates the times as allowed in the working timetable for November 1946.

Due to the poor quality of the coal available it was not easy to convert it into briquettes, although a few second-hand briquetting plants were acquired in the spring of 1942. These were worked non-stop every day, and in the first six months had produced 30,000 tons of briquetted fuel, after which the output was raised to 80,000 tons per annum. Arising from the scarcity of coal, smokebox ash was sometimes incorporated in the briquettes, thus lowering the calorific value of the completed product. Other alternative fuels tried were Irish coal, phurnacite, pulverised coal, ordinary turf and briquetted turf. Irish coal had not been previously used. It had a high ash content, varying from 15% to 30% and a volatile content ranging from 10% to 20%. In combination with pitch it was, however, used for fire lighting. Phurnacite, a high carbon fuel, was intended mainly for enclosed smokeless stoves. It gave a good bright fire, but the supply was limited and prices high.

Pulverised coal was one of the more interesting experiments. It was apparently akin to oil burning. The tender contained this fuel in a very fine powdered form, from which it was displaced into a small diameter pipe partly by gravity and partly by a worm working in the bottom of the hopper. It entered a larger pipe which it met at right angles, through which a jet of air passed, then through a flexible coupling between the tender and the locomotive. Under the footplate, the pipe continued until it entered the bottom of the firebox, which was brick lined, at ashpan level. The fuel was then blown through a circular plate containing hundreds of small holes. It was lighted by throwing in a small piece of waste or merely by allowing the fuel jet to play upon the remains of the wood fire which was used to raise the boiler pressure to about 50psi, or just sufficient to work the essential auxiliaries such as the air fan. Its steaming properties were reported to be truly remarkable. However the technical disadvantages outweighed the advantages and, after careful consideration, the experiment was discontinued.

To appreciate the value of turf in locomotive use, it is only necessary to analyse a dried sample. It has a volatile content of 71%, fixed carbon 24.5% and ash 4.5%. The excessive volatile content, which might on first consideration have been the solution to the company's problems, burnt readily so when the demand for extra steam arose the consumption rate was so high, even in a medium-sized engine, that it was impossible to maintain steam. In addition it required an auxiliary tender and extra staff, and its use caused lengthy delays. Briquetted turf, with its higher bulk-density figure, was more favourable, but it was not available in large quantities and was expensive. Briquetted turf had a moisture content of around 20% compared to a figure ranging from 28% to

40% for ordinary turf. Some briquetted turf had a moisture content as low as 12% but this was probably exceptional. Consumption of turf briquettes was also high, although it was used with some success on the D&SE section suburban services towards the end of the war.

It would be wrong to suggest that these various forms of special fuels completely solved the transport problem, simply because they were available only in limited quantities. For example, in the year 1943, the GSR used 306,000 tons of fuel of all kinds. Of this figure, only about 30% represented alternative fuels. Delays, some serious, occurred but timekeeping had improved vastly over 1942. Constant attention was required in the testing and analysis of fuel. Five categories of fuel were recognised, the premier category (grade A), mainly phurnacite, briquettes and other coals, being used for passenger services, heavy goods trains received grade B, lighter goods grade C and so on. One can only imagine what grade E fuel was like.

Various tests are briefly referred to in connection with the use of turf. For example, in July 1942, Father Murphy, Parish Priest of Borris wrote to the company offering a small consignment of "conventional turf" in addition to a hard, black, turf product known locally as "Crutans". The asking price of 50s per ton was, however, regarded as being exceptionally high. Nevertheless, a trial was carried out on the Bagenalstown to Palace East section on 4th August, consumption working out at a staggering 149.3lb per mile. The engine (unidentified but probably a 101 class 0-6-0) was reported to have steamed satisfactorily, and to have maintained time. It was estimated that the cost of working was increased 50% on normal coal usage, and no further purchases were made of this product.

The TDB supplied a consignment of 50 tons of turf briquettes from Lullymore in Co. Kildare in July 1942 and arrangements were made for trials to be carried out on the 17.10 goods ex-Kingsbridge. The engine concerned was 321 or D3 class 4-4-0 No 329. Nearly seven tons of turf was loaded on to the locomotive's own tender, with a further seven tons on a second tender. This fuel was consumed over a mileage of 292 miles, consumption working out at 107lb per mile. The balance of the consignment was mixed with duff and proved useful. However, when the company made enquiries as to purchasing a further consignment, they were informed that all of the output of briquettes from Lullymore went to Fuel Importers Ltd for distribution to the poorer classes in Dublin.

Another test of which we have details, was the working of a train of turf wagons or carriages (during the war years, old six-wheeled carriages were converted to carry turf) both ways between Kingsbridge and Portarlington in February 1944 with 333 or D4 class 4-4-0 No 339. The load on the down run was nine empty turf vehicles, the return journey being with six laden "turf carriages", a very small load for the engine in question. Consumption on this occasion worked out

FUEL PROBLEMS DURING THE 1940s

GNR(I) Qs 4-4-0 No 133, similar to QLs No 127 used in the July 1941 turf-burning trials. This latter engine returned turf/coal consumption figures varying from 50 to 67 lbs per mile.

(G Beesley collection)

at 81.6lb per mile, and the engine was reported to have steamed well with no trouble experienced. The Northern District Locomotive Superintendent, who was in charge of this trial, considered that the briquettes would, however, be better employed in steam-raising as they would provide a clean fire starting out from shed, and there would be no problems with inadequate tender capacity.

In relation to the D&SE section suburban working referred to above, C.F. Tyndall, the Running Superintendent, reported to Bredin on experiments carried out on the Harcourt Street to Bray line during the month of July 1944. Once again, consumption was high, working out at 100lb per mile over a period of four weeks, an increase of 25lb per mile over the poor quality coal then in use. This represented an increase of eighty-six tons per week, or an increase of about £300 per week in monetary terms. Reference was made to the increased risk of fire and the necessity for all members of staff to be continually on the alert to prevent possible serious loss to rolling stock, apart from the risk to adjoining third party property. Fires were a problem with the use of turf, and instructions had been issued in July 1942 that engines confined to branch lines, using turf or timber exclusively as fuel, were to be fitted without delay with openings at the top of the smokebox with cover plates controlled from the cab. Tyndall summarised by stating that turf briquettes could be used where the mileage between depots was not excessive; consumption was however out of proportion to the work done.

The TDB wrote in December 1944 suggesting that economies might be effected by making certain permanent alterations to locomotives, for example, changes in grate arrangements and the fitting of spark arrestors. The company replied that no substantial reductions had been made. Experiments had been carried out involving C2 4-4-2T No 455, initially fitted with an extended blast pipe. When fitted with a spark arrestor, consumption increased by about 20%. The arrestor in question consisted of a perforated sheet iron cone, extending from the base of the chimney to within 2in of the top of the blast pipe. This had the effect of reducing steaming capacity and it was found necessary to provide air ducts with a controlled air inlet under the firebars.

By an Act of the Oireachtas passed in 1944, the GSR was amalgamated with the Dublin United Tramways Company to form Córas Iompair Éireann as from 1st January 1945, which latter was nationalised in 1950, taking under its wing the Grand Canal Company. It is perhaps of interest to mention that CIE used 70,000 tons more coal in 1945 to work a service of four million miles less than in 1939. Corresponding fuel costs were £1 million in 1945 as against £334,000 in 1939. It was without doubt, a great tribute to the drivers and firemen that services were maintained as they were throughout the war years. The situation was only just beginning to improve post-war when nature intervened to further disrupt the railways.

The winter of 1946/7 proved to be one of the worst

11

in living memory, with severe frosts and heavy snowfalls, resulting in severe restrictions on the importation of coal, which could not be moved from the collieries in Great Britain. This had an almost immediate effect. As from Monday 20th January 1947, both passenger and goods trains were altered to run on four days per week, the passenger service consisting of only one train in each direction on each of the main lines on the four days in question. The circular however pointed out that the continuance of the services, both passenger and goods, would depend on the amount of coal available; it was stipulated that shunting at stations should be reduced to a minimum. Passenger services on many of the branch lines were discontinued as from the following Monday, while on other sections, those trains which did operate became mixed. Within a month, these services were being further restricted to three days weekly. Four-day services were resumed on Saturday 24th May 1947. These restrictions in coal supply led to the conversion of a number of engines to burn yet another fuel, namely oil, and we shall shortly take a look at this.

GNR(I) Wartime Experiments with Turf

The GNR(I) suffered similar problems of shortage and poor quality of conventional fuels during the War years as far as the Republic was concerned. Depots in Northern Ireland continued to use coal throughout the War. On 11th July 1940, the Chief Mechanical Engineer, H. McIntosh, reported the out-shopping of T2 class 4-4-2T No 142 fitted with pyrometers etc, with the intention that it would commence burning turf on the following Monday. The engine was to be regarded as a travelling laboratory, with initial experiments to be "of the broadest possible nature and intended to give preliminary information only". He did also state, however, that the Drawing Office at Dundalk had already prepared plans for slight modifications to standard firebars and to blast pipe and chimney arrangements.

Initially, fifty tons of turf were ordered from the TDB. This followed an examination of a sample from Donegal, which was reported to be exceptionally well-dried turf with a good calorific value. Some turf from Ballinagh in Co. Cavan was also tested, but was found to be inferior to the Donegal product. On receipt of the first twenty tons of the above order, tests showed that some of it was of considerably poorer quality and rather wetter than expected. It is not entirely clear, but it appears that no turf-burning tests were carried out during 1940, although in January of the following year, consideration was given to obtaining 3,000 tons of turf from Clonsast Bog near Portarlington. This turf was to be delivered via the GSR at Amiens Street for 27s 3d per ton.

Some 300 tons of this consignment had reached the railway by 11th February and was reported to compare very unfavourably with supplies received from Turraun Bog (part of the Boora system, three miles from Ferbane, Co. Offaly). This variation in quality clearly indicates the difficulties in obtaining a regular supply of good quality turf. The Clonsast

turf would be difficult to fire, and due to the very low bulk density (143cu ft per ton as against 95 for the turf supplied in 1940), the tender capacity would be low. McIntosh wrote to the TDB stating that the railway required good, dense, well-humified turf. If this was not available, it was suggested that execution of the order be delayed. As a consequence, the TDB agreed to suspend delivery. The GSR had been incurring similar problems with their supplies as witnessed by a memorandum from Ginnety to Meadows in March 1942. H. A. Massey, the Superintendent of the Locomotive Department in Cork, had inspected a consignment of turf at Skibbereen but thought it unfit for locomotive use, it being in a very sodden condition and of a very soft nature. In fact, a representative of the Urban District Council informed Massey that the reason they had the turf on offer at all was that the local people considered it to be of poor quality, and would not purchase it.

Towards the end of March 1941, McIntosh again wrote to the TDB pointing out that the experiments were at a standstill due to the lack of suitable turf. He also wrote to his General Manager, George Howden, suggesting the disposal of the unsuitable turf locally or to the company's hotels. Howden, in due course, confirmed that the board had sanctioned the distribution of this turf to the company's hotels and stations in the Republic. At the same time, Howden wrote to a certain C.S. Andrews, then Managing Director of the TDB, but in later years as Chairman of CIE to be closely associated with the closure of many of the CIE lines, asking if anything could be done to obtain supplies of good quality turf. Andrews replied offering 3,000 tons from Donegal.

So to 7th July 1941, when Locomotive Inspector R Green submitted a report of a trial four days earlier with locomotive No 142 between Dundalk and Dublin and return. The empty carriage train, equal to six small coaches, made the ordinary stops of a local passenger train on the up journey between Dundalk and Donabate, with four station stops on the return journey. The consumption of Turraun turf for this work was 71lb per mile, including 6cwt for lighting up, or 65lb per mile for actual train working. The engine was reported to have steamed very well throughout, maintaining a firebed of about 3in in spite of the rapid firing rate. The turf used was hard and close grained, broken up into a convenient size, mostly about the size of a half brick.

On the 4th July, 4-4-0 tender engine No 127 of QLs class was provided with five boxes of Turraun turf weighing 22½cwt, the remainder of the tender holding coal. No 127 worked the 12.25 up local train between Dundalk and Drogheda fired only on turf. The train was equivalent to 8½ small coaches and the engine steamed exceptionally well, with an estimated consumption of 67lb per mile. At Drogheda, the remaining 9cwt of turf were mixed with about 5cwt of slack coal, and the train was worked on to Dublin with this mixture, averaging 50lb per mile, again with excellent steaming results.

FUEL PROBLEMS DURING THE 1940s

Five days later it was the turn of S2 4-4-0 No 190 "Lugnaquilla", again on the 12.25 up from Dundalk. Her tender (one of the 3,500 gallon type) was filled with 58½cwt of Turraun turf. She had a load of 102 tons (6½ small coaches), consumption being 55lb per mile, and once again the engine steamed well. The engine returned to Dundalk on the 17.30 down local with 186 tons as far as Drogheda and 153¼ tons on to Dundalk. A mixture of 27cwt of turf and 9cwt of coal was used which resulted, after weighing off 12cwt, in a consumption of 49.54lb per mile. Inspector Green commented that the capacity of the tender would only be sufficient to carry turf to work the round trip from Dundalk to Dublin, a distance of about 100 miles. He also commented that, even with this better class of turf, the rate of firing was still high requiring practically continuous firing, and it would be doubtful whether one fireman could adequately work such a train. It was for this reason that Green had arranged for the mixture of coal and turf. He offered the view that if turf were to be adopted as a fuel, it would be necessary to build in a substantial extension in timing, coupled with the keeping of loads within reasonable limits.

Further supplies of turf were ordered from Donegal. Reporting in September 1941 on the results to date, Mr T. Bratt from the Laboratory in Dundalk stated that the initial tests were sufficiently encouraging to permit the use of turf on certain services. Whereas the Turraun turf consumption averaged 71lb per mile with good steaming, firing was so rapid as to raise serious doubts as to whether such fuel on its own was capable of being handled by one fireman. Clonsast turf was quite a different matter with consumption working out at 106lb per mile, including lighting up. The firing was continuous and at times it was necessary for both the driver and the fireman to attend to firing simultaneously. There was a tendency, due to the light nature of the fuel, to lift the firebed badly, indicating the necessity for better blast control.

Despite these drawbacks, Bratt was of the opinion, given suitable equipment and an adequate supply of good quality turf, that it should be possible to carry on certain services with turf only. Certain modifications would be required to engines, including the provision of a means for varying the intensity of the draught at will, so that it would not be dependent on the amount of exhaust steam entering the chimney at any one time. In addition, there should be provision of preheated secondary air ensuring better combining of the air and gas mixtures. He concluded his report by stating that arrangements were being worked out for the equipping of one locomotive in the near future; no such alterations were made. However, Bratt was clearly thinking along the same lines as Bulleid would on CIE in the not too distant future.

Back on the GSR, Bredin wrote in May 1942 to the CME's office at Inchicore asking them to arrange to provide McIntosh with a plan and side elevation of a 101 class engine coupled to a large tender, showing the footplate dimensions in detail. It was reported that McIntosh was in course of preparing a conveyor for turf firing and was arranging to adapt it to suit a 101 class engine, and was prepared to loan the plant to the GSR when available. Ginnety was also requested to forward ten tons of duff and one ton of pitch to Dundalk, being careful to ensure that, for safety reasons, the pitch was placed under the duff. McIntosh was handed the relevant drawings during the course of a visit to Inchicore at the end of May. Despite a number of reminders regarding the conveyor, it is not clear whether the GSR ever received one on loan or otherwise from Dundalk. We do know that difficulties were encountered in acquiring suitable bearings for the engine portion.

As an aside, it is worth mentioning that the GNR(I) made contact in June 1943 with Messrs Nydquist & Holm AB of Denmark, who had successfully supplied steam turbine locomotives to Argentina and Sweden on the Ljüngströms principle. Probably due to the War nothing further transpired although Dundalk turned their attention to gas turbines during 1946, believing these offered greater possibilities than steam turbines. Brown Boveri pointed out that the smallest viable locomotive in terms of thermal efficiency would be of 2,500hp. They offered such an A1A-A1A unit with a total weight of 112½ tons, the maximum axle load being 18¾ tons, and with a maximum speed of 90mph. The price complete and ready for service was quoted at £100,000 with a delivery of three years. Howden advised McIntosh that the cost was altogether prohibitive and enquired what a similar machine on order by the Great Western Railway (later to become British Railways No 18000, delivered in 1949) would cost. McIntosh confirmed a similar figure and here the question of turbine traction for an Irish railway died.

Before leaving the GNR(I), reference should be made to the difficulties encountered with fuel supplies during 1944. On 12th May, a deputation from the GNR(I) had an interview with Messrs Andrews and Williams of the TDB along with Miss Thekla Beere of the Department of Supplies. At the meeting, they advised that special precautions had been taken prior to the restriction of supplies to build up a stock of locomotive coal in Northern Ireland and Éire – about 32,000 tons. Of this figure, the supply south of the Border as of 6th May stood at 7,513 tons, a reserve of about 12 weeks even with the much reduced services being operated. In the company's view, stocks should not in any circumstances be allowed to drop below 2,350 tons, sufficient for four to five weeks.

However, the Government was now asking that the company divert some of its weekly deliveries to the Electricity Supply Board generating station at the Pigeon House in Dublin. The company expressed their serious reservations at this request, as such reductions might have grave consequences for their operations, but it would be of comparatively minor benefit to other users. They strongly urged that they should not be asked to forego more than 400 tons per week during a period of eight weeks, after which time they would expect normal deliveries.

BULLEID AND THE TURF BURNER

One further road test is mentioned. Inspector Green reported on a test run on 6th June with QL 4-4-0 No 156 working the 07.35 local from Dublin to Dundalk using briquetted turf supplied by Fuel Importers Ltd. The load was of five bogies and seven four-wheeled trucks, equivalent to eleven six-wheeled coaches. The weather was reported to be stormy. The train ran to the scheduled running times, and the engine steamed well with a consumption of 92.9lb per mile. At the end of the run, there was a residue of brownish ash with small pieces of clinker. The consumption compared with an average of 70lb per mile for poor quality coal currently being used in Éire (an increase of 32.8%), steaming qualities being much better and involving less labour. As the result of this test, McIntosh wrote to Howden recommending without hesitation, if costs permitted, that any coal being received in Éire should be exchanged for briquettes.

About a week after this test, the Department of Supplies wrote stating that they would be prepared to let the company have up to 37,000 tons of briquettes in return for their current stocks of coal along with future deliveries. The 'barter' was to be made on the basis of 1¼ tons of briquettes for every ton of coal, which McIntosh thought on the low side. Tests carried out on turf supplies at Merchants' Warehouse at the East Wall in Dublin showed that some of it was not up to the standard of the sample supplied. Nevertheless the company started taking delivery of briquettes on 19th June.

McIntosh submitted a further report to Howden on 21st August pointing out the advantages of the briquettes over the poor quality coal which had led to frequent disorganisation of services due to bad steaming and prolonged stops to remove clinker and ash from fireboxes – similar problems to those encountered by the GSR. Briquetted turf had some disadvantages, however, and these included increased consumption, emission of sparks from the chimney causing lineside and carriage roof fires, disintegration of turf when exposed to weather and the bunker space, which worked out at about one-third less in favour of coal. To introduce extensive alterations in the design and fittings of engines to get the best advantages from turf would present difficulties in view of the fact that engines stationed in Éire might be required to work into Northern Ireland and use coal. Arrangements had already been made to reduce the airspace between the firebars and, where possible, to extend the brick arches. A number of spark arrestors had been fitted but the design had proved to be insufficiently effective to prevent spark emission. The barter arrangement came to an end in October 1944, at which time deliveries of turf had fallen way below the comparative supplies of coal to the ESB.

D4 class 4-4-0 No 344 at Cork running shed. No 346 of this class spent some time during 1947 on the GNR(I) on exchange trials, equipped as an oil-burner.
(H. Fayle, courtesy IRRS)

4

AN ALTERNATIVE FUEL IS TRIED

A brief description of the different oil-burning conversions for steam locomotives would be useful at this point in our narrative, in particular, the two principal types in use in Ireland. Broadly speaking, there are four types of conversion for oil-burning. The Weir type, as largely used by CIE, was so named from the fact that the oil flowed over a weir. The annular jet type, largely used in ships and power houses, consisted of concentric jets of steam and oil. The Laidlaw Drew system was incorporated in the GNR(I) locomotives converted to burn oil, while the fourth type was known as the Hardy system, and was claimed to overcome inherent difficulties with other forms of burner. By their nature, steam locomotives present complex draught problems, due to the air intake varying with the speed of the train, load hauled, varying cut-off and the nature of the lineside, for example in a cutting, on an embankment, etc. These variations can be quite different for different classes of locomotive, so it can be appreciated that there are many factors in play when considering conversion to oil.

Briefly, in the Weir system as used by CIE, the tender held approximately 1,400 gallons of fuel oil, which was fed by gravity through a flexible coupling to what in a conventional locomotive would be referred to as the ashpan. On the opposite side to the oil inlet on the burner, there was a live steam inlet controlled from the footplate. The burner itself was mounted on studs set into the bottom of the foundation ring, and was adjustable both laterally and vertically to a limited extent. The burner actually faced the fire hole door, but of course the flame was directed somewhat lower. To light an oil burner, burning waste was thrown into the firebox, and the steam jet turned on, followed by the oil. The steam quickly atomised the oil, which was projected across the bricked floor of the firebox and instantly ignited. Whilst the ashpan was airtight, it was fitted with a conventional damper which controlled the ingress of air. There were three square openings in the bricked floor, about 10in square in the larger locomotives, the air being drawn through these by the normal vacuum created by the exhaust action.

The Laidlaw Drew system differed in that the burner was located on the floor of the firebox and the oil was discharged at an upward angle. The air inlets were circular in form and were arranged tangentially around the burner, so that the incoming air, meeting the burning atomised oil as it emerged from the burner, caused the gases to swirl in a Catherine Wheel pattern. There was little or no direct impingement on the brick work or firebox plates, a decided advantage from the point of view of maintenance.

The first reference to oil being used in an Irish locomotive that the author has been able to trace was on the narrow-gauge Tralee & Dingle Railway in Co. Kerry. Their locomotive No 5, a 2-6-2T from Messrs Hunslet, was delivered in 1892, and was fitted as new with Holden oil-burning apparatus. This proved so economical that further sets were ordered from the manufacturers for fitting to the company's 2-6-0 tanks. However for some strange reason these were never fitted, and in fact, No 5 was converted to coal firing in 1893, presumably due to difficulties in obtaining oil fuel. CIE had briefly carried out some experiments with oil-burning in March 1945, but these were stopped due to the general non-availability of fuel oil at that time. The tests were only carried out at all due to oil being provided on a 'limited licence' basis. Authorisation for the conversion of a 257 class engine was given at a meeting between the General Manager, E.C. Bredin, who as CME had been responsible for the design of the 800 class 4-6-0 locomotives, J.J. Johnston, the Chief Draughtsman, and G.H. Burnell, the Chief Chemist, on 2nd March.

Reporting on 30th May, the Running Superintendent, C.F. Tyndall, stated that engine No 264 had by then completed 754 miles as an oil-burner, with an average consumption of 4.7 gallons per mile. It had completed three trips each on light and heavy oil. Steaming was reported to be satisfactory with the former, but not so good with the heavy oil due to an imperfect oil/air mixture. It was estimated that to do the same work as a ton of coal, approximately 200 gallons of heavy oil were required. Whilst it was recognised that there would be staff savings in coal handling and fire lighting, the burning of fuel oil tended to shorten the life of fireboxes and tubes. At the end of 1945, the company reported details of the experiments to the Department for Industry & Commerce and requested that oil supplies be made available. The initial response in March 1946 was that the Government could not give oil to the company from the limited quantities of fuel oil available. However, six months later, CIE received an allocation of 6,000 gallons of fuel oil and No 264 went into regular goods service on Monday 16th September 1946.

Tyndall reported to Frank Lemass, who had succeeded Bredin as General Manager, in November 1946 on complaints from the Traffic Department on the deterioration in timekeeping of both passenger and goods trains. In addition, the coal consumption had increased on average 10lb per mile during the previous month, varying from 90lb per mile to 128.8lb. The fuel crisis in the latter part of 1946 came on almost without warning and it was fortunate that the trials with No 264 had taken place. Immediate authorisation was given for the conversion of "two decent-sized locomotives - one goods and one passenger" to burn oil. The Department for Industry & Commerce wrote on 27th November offering to make available 25,000 tons of heavy oil during the first half of 1947.

At this point, the average consumption for No 264 was working out at 5.36 gallons per mile, which at 7¼d per gallon equalled 38.86d per mile. Other engines in the same class were averaging 39.98d per mile with coal, this latter costing 66s 8d per ton. Matters now moved swiftly as witnessed by a letter from Lemass to Tyndall stating that in view of the deterioration in the quality of coal and, more importantly, the difficulty in securing supplies, it was necessary to consider the conversion of between 30 and 40 engines to burn oil by the end of March 1947. Tyndall replied that he should have about 30 engines converted in the time allocated at an average cost of £350 per engine. He went on to say that arrangements were being made to convert engines of classes 333 (4-4-0), 372 (2-6-0) and 623 (0-6-0).

By 26th February, Tyndall was able to report that a 372 class 2-6-0 (Woolwich) was saving about 60 tons of coal per week based on a single Kingsbridge to Cork working. It was suggested that a double trip daily might be possible with some recasting of the timetable, but this suggestion was not followed up. Conversions proved to be slower than anticipated, only thirteen having been completed by 22nd March, with only eight of these at work, six on the Southern and two on the Midland. Towards the end of April, Lemass had reason to comment that he was, "not at all satisfied that the best use is being made of the availability of these locomotives". Instructions were now given for the conversion of a further twenty engines. The notion of double tripping was knocked on the head by the Traffic Department in May when it was pointed out that six hours in every twenty-four were required for watering, fuelling, turning etc. The average distance covered by a goods train in nine hours was only about eighty miles and it would not therefore be feasible to operate double trips other than to Athlone or Longford from Dublin.

At a meeting on 14th May, J.H. Dudley, the Assistant Running Superintendent, reported that when the conversion of the balance of the heavy goods engines was complete, all goods engines with comparatively large fireboxes would have been dealt with, and they would then have to consider those with smaller fireboxes. The question was whether the company should install their own type of burner or the Laidlaw-Drew type as used on the GNR(I). The most suitable locomotives remaining for conversion consisted of about 96 of the 101 class and 34 of the 593 type in the goods fleet and about 16 of the 321 and 333 class passenger engines. Instructions were given for the conversion of the remaining twelve heavy goods engines. One of the 101s was to receive a Laidlaw-Drew burner and one the company's own (Weir) type for comparison. Pending the results of these tests, work was to proceed on the passenger engines suggested by Dudley.

Dudley reported in July on the result of the trial with No 255 (the 101 class fitted with the Weir burner) and whilst it had proved satisfactory, he urged caution in converting a small number of the class as they were used widely for beet and grain traffic in season. They would be left "orphaned" due to lack of oil storage bases away from their normal routes. It would be preferable to convert the 573 and 594

classes which seldom strayed from the Midland section. Dudley also commented on difficulties in maintenance of the oil-burners due to searing of crown stays as the result of the high temperatures encountered. He was arranging to borrow a GNR(I) engine fitted with a Laidlaw-Drew burner for trials on the D&SE section. No details were given of the locomotive concerned or of the results of the experiments. We do however know that D4 4-4-0 No 346 was loaned for a short while to the GNR(I). It was not until the third week in October 1947 that Tyndall was able to report the completion of the 101 class with the Laidlaw-Drew burner. Delays had resulted from insufficient drawings being supplied by the manufacturers. This burner required care in its use and adequate crew training, the GNR(I) having experienced several explosions in the firebox.

Towards the end of November 1947, the company took stock of its experiments with oil-burning. Whilst there were undoubted advantages, there were also several serious disadvantages to be considered. Coal supplies were expected to return to normal in the near future, and this fact had to be considered against the conversion costs, additional maintenance, the backlog of normal overhaul due to the conversion programme, and the provision of oil supply facilities at various locations. The following facts emerged for early consideration:

[1] Under the existing conditions, it was clear that the avowed policy of complete conversion to diesel-electric power would have to be postponed for an indefinite period of years. The inference from this was that steam traction must be continued longer than contemplated.

[2] According to locomotive class, conversion to oil-burning cost £400 to £500 per locomotive plus the cost of many and widespread storage tanks.

[3] Questions were raised as to whether it might be better to purchase locomotives complete to cover the interim period, to rely on re-boilering the existing stock, or a combination of both. Attention should perhaps also be directed to whether any improvements in design might be introduced which would enable better use to be made of British and Irish coals if modernisation was impracticable. Almost immediately, instructions were issued for a stop to be made to further conversions, apart from those already in hand.

An interesting aside came to light in January 1948, when a letter of complaint was received from a resident in Whitworth Road in Glasnevin, Dublin, stating that for some weeks past a few of the trains passing along the adjoining line had been shaking the house very much. He reported that two side walls had been badly split and a new ceiling put up about twelve months previously had also split across. Tyndall sent the letter to Lemass for legal opinion, pointing out that whilst oil-burning was not specifically mentioned in the letter, he believed that it was inferred. It was a fact that high frequency vibration was almost inseparable from the use of oil-burning engines. In due course, Counsel confirmed that the company would not be liable for any damage so caused.

In all, 93 engines were converted to burn oil. The cost had been £38,890 for the work on the engines, £10,117 for mobile tankers and £34,876 for fuel oil storage. The cost of re-conversion was £5,068. The work of re-conversion commenced in February 1948, and it was hoped to convert a minimum of 10 by the end of March, followed by six units per week after that. See Appendix E for details of mileages, etc for the fleet during 1947. However, the Laidlaw-Drew conversion, No 185 was retained for a little while longer for further tests. She ran from Dublin to Cork with a load of 45 wagons, returning a fuel consumption of 3.83 gallons per mile with an actual running time of 8 hours and 8 minutes. In all, she ran about 30,000 miles as an oil- burner. The final chapter in the oil-burning story was the conversion of 101 class No 197 in 1954 with an improved Laidlaw-Drew burner. As oil-burning engines were not so prone to breakdowns and delays, a large white circle was painted on the smokebox door and on the tender sides of these engines so that signalmen could give preference to them in traffic.

any improvement. Hinchcliffe referred to the 550,000 miles or 22 years criteria for boiler replacement, and it was estimated that there was a requirement for 112 boilers at a unit cost of £2,500, giving an estimated cost of £280,000. The report also included an interesting review of the various engine classes extant in 1946, which is included as Appendix A. Quotations had been obtained from five outside builders as below and Hinchcliffe urged a positive response from the board.

Supplier	Delivery	Z class	K class
Vulcan Foundry F.O.B. Liverpool.	Oct 1948 & 6 per month	10 @ £2,295 each 20 @ £2,195 each 50 @ £2,144 each	10 @ £3,378 each
Carbomet, Brussels F.O.B. Antwerp	2-3 months & 4 per month	12 @ £2,498 each 24 @ £2,460 each 50 @ £2,435 each	12 @ £3,825 each 24 @ £3,364 each 50 @ £3,741 each
Hudswell Clarke F.A.S. Liverpool	Jan. 1949 & 1 per month	10 @ £2,741 each 20 @ £2,683 each 50 @ £2,653 each	
Baldwin, Philadelphia	10 in 9 months & 5 per week thereafter	10 @ £3,054 each 20 @ £2,854 each 50 @ £2,741 each (plus £214 freight, insurance)	10 @ £4,445 each 20 @ £4,197 each 50 @ £4,049 each (plus £450 freight, insurance)
Czechoslovak Eng. Works, Prague. F.O.B. Rotterdam	9 months & 5 per month	50 @ £5,250 each (amended to £3,460)	

A large order for boilers

Tyndall wrote to Lemass in October 1946 outlining the boiler situation at that time. As of 24th March of that year there were 548 boilers and 461 locomotives, that is 87 or 18.87% spare boilers. Tyndall stated that the recognised economic life of a boiler was 550,000 miles or 22 years. The average mileage in the years preceding 1946 was more than 650,000. In fact a 101 type boiler in locomotive No 93 was 34 years old and had accumulated 876,000 miles, and one of the Bandon tanks had 722,000 miles on its boiler. This was largely due to the effects of the War years.

Moving ahead nearly a year, R.T. Hinchcliffe, the Production Manager, wrote at length to the General Manager on 4th September 1947 on the subject of boilers following representations to him by Tyndall. Hinchcliffe reported that he had fully investigated the position and his findings were "somewhat alarming". Unless immediate action was taken to obtain replacement boilers from outside sources, the company would "experience a complete breakdown with the operation of steam locomotives". The existing facilities at Inchicore could in no way meet the situation, and even the introduction of a night shift, which would be dependent on obtaining sufficient skilled labour, would not alleviate matters. Materials that had been ordered as long ago as August 1945 remained undelivered, and there was little prospect of

Matters now moved quickly and Lemass replied on 19th September requesting that enquiries be sent out for complete boilers of the quantity and type recommended, viz:

Class C	22
Class D	10
Class K	8
Class N	12
Class Q	2
Class W	8
Class Z	50

a total of 112. Lemass went on to comment that "owing to the multiplicity of type of locomotive with which the Company is burdened, I trust you will keep foremost in mind the question of reducing the number of types as much as possible by eliminating the least suitable type of locomotive and concentrating our efforts on those locomotives, which we feel would give us the most service".

BULLEID AND THE TURF BURNER

Hinchcliffe wrote back to Lemass on 24th November 1947, enclosing details of three quotations (see below), that of the Vulcan Foundry of Newton-le-Willows being favoured. The other two contenders, Hudswell Clarke of Leeds and Carbomet of Brussels, were only prepared to quote for one and two types of boiler respectively. Alternative quotes had been obtained for the fitting of monel metal firebox stays in place of copper, the former having distinct advantages in service, which would more than off set the price difference. Hinchcliffe was requested to examine further the tenders received on a 'survival basis', that is that boilers should be purchased for locomotives likely to survive. He was also advised that it was probable that the company would obtain about 34 diesel-electric locomotives of approximately 1,500 hp each by the end of 1950, and also that some alternative source of motive power for the operation of suburban services would be in sight at about the same time.

on the basis of one per week commencing in August 1949, with 25 Z class up to February 1950, followed by the 6 Ks between August and October 1950, the remainder to be delivered between February 1951 and May 1952. It was not stipulated in which order the remaining 63 boilers would be delivered.

J.H. Dudley, the Assistant Running Superintendent, wrote on 13th May 1948, expressing his concerns at the boiler situation. Not only were the engines whose boiler life was expended a serious difficulty, but they were also adversely affecting the whole standard of repair, because boiler life was becoming an increasing factor in determining when general repairs were due to engines, not mileage. High mileage engines were thus remaining in service. Of the engines in service, 36 were on boiler time limit, although 9 of these had less than 60,000 miles. Dudley cited the 372/393 (Woolwich) class position. The 26 engines in these classes were vital, as

Class	Vulcan Foundry			Hudswell Clarke	Carbomet
	Quantity	Copper	Monel	Each	Each
C	22	£61,446	£63,668		
K	8	£30,320	£31,452		
N	12	£34,536	£35,748		£4,208*
Q	2	£7540	£7,784		
W	8	£26,768	£27,744		
Z	50	£117,100	£121,225	£2,720**	£2,680***
D	10	£33,380	£34,565		
Total	112	£311,090	£322,186		
Material		BSS	BSS	BSS	SNCB Spec
Delivery Commence		First quarter 1950	First quarter 1950	December 1949	Early 1949
Rate		6 per month	6 per month	1 per 6 weeks	4 per month
Delivery		F.O.B. Liverpool	F.O.B. Liverpool	As Vulcan	F.O.B. Antwerp
Notes	* 12 quoted for	** 10 quoted for	*** 50 quoted for		

Having considered the matter, it was decided to delete the two Q class and reduce classes C and W respectively by ten and four, thus reducing the total to 96. In the event, only six K boilers were ordered, bringing the total number to 94. Having sought some price reductions, Vulcan agreed to reduce the unit cost on the Z boilers, the total quote being £261,227. The order was formally confirmed for 94 boilers on 10th January 1948, and it was agreed that deliveries would be

they were the largest engines capable of working various lines. Only 15 were in service, and only 5 of these were reported as being in good condition, the boiler life of the class being almost expended. Complete failures to boilers represented 27% of all failures for the first three months of the year and if oil-burning engines, which were agreed to be abnormal, were removed from the equation, the situation was even worse with 33% of remaining failures down to boilers.

AN ALTERNATIVE FUEL IS TRIED

On Saturday 7th May there were 80 engines stopped in various sheds for repair, while on Tuesday 10th May after the departure of the 10.00 Cork passenger, there was not a single passenger engine on shed in Inchicore. Dudley stressed the necessity to provide generally improved conditions for carrying out repairs. We shall return to the question of boilers a little later in our narrative.

No 386 depicted whilst running as an oil-burner in the late 1940s. One of 93 engines converted at this time, the system worked reasonably well, and certainly assisted in alleviating the chronic coal crisis that existed at that time. The large white circles were carried by all the oil-burners and indicated to signalmen that this particular working was hauled by an engine that was oil-fired, and did not therefore need to be sidetracked to clean the fire or raise steam. Such workings were thus allowed to run unhindered.

A somewhat creased, but nevertheless pleasing, view of Light Pacific No 21C164, photographed when new outside Brighton Works in July 1947. She was later renumbered 34064 and named "Fighter Command". Bulleid is in the back row, eighth from left, immediately beneath the front of the cab. Note the patent Boxpok wheels.

(Southern Railway official)

Bulleid's SR Leader Class 0-6-6-0 No 36001 alongside the Eastleigh coaling stage on 16th August 1950. Certain similarities with CC1 can be seen in this photograph. One big advantage of Leader over CC1 was the fitting of driving cabs at the locomotive's outer ends. As referred to on page 23, there is a suggestion that CIE were considering the purchase of the five engines of this type after BR decided to abandon work on the project.

(J.H Ashton)

5

O.V.S. BULLEID AND THE LEADER PROJECT

The brothers John and William Bulleid emigrated from their native Devon to New Zealand in 1875. William settled in the South Island at Invercargill, where he set up in business. Such was his success, that William returned to England on a business voyage only three years later. Whilst home in England, he met a friend, Marianne Vaughan Pugh, whom he married. and the couple returned to New Zealand in the autumn of 1878. Their first of three children, Oliver Vaughan Snell, was born on 19th September 1882. Only seven years later, tragedy struck the family when Oliver's father contracted pleurisy and died. The family moved to stay with John Bulleid at Oamaru; less than a year after William's death however, plans were made for the family to return to Britain.

At first, the Bulleids settled down with Marianne's family at Llanfyllin on the old Cambrian Railways. Just before his tenth birthday, young Oliver was sent off to boarding school in Scotland. Rather than returning home after his final year, Oliver was then sent to stay with his Aunt Janet in Lancashire as a companion for her son Vaughan. Oliver duly attended Accrington Technical School, where he excelled in a number of subjects, leaving there in 1899 at the age of seventeen. At this stage, the intention appears to have been that he should return to New Zealand to join his Uncle John in business there. Fate, however, intervened to shape his future, and his Aunt Janet dispatched him to another cousin, the Reverend Edgar Lee, who lived near Doncaster. Lee was high church Anglican, and probably arising from this, Oliver later converted to Catholicism. It was reported that on his first day at Inchicore, he bought a crucifix, which was duly hung up in his office. To celebrate Marian Year in 1954, the men in the Works at Inchicore came up with the idea of erecting a statue to the Blessed Virgin. Bulleid was approached and readily gave his approval. Subsequently, Mass was celebrated annually in the Works on one of the major Feast Days.

The Reverend Lee suggested that Oliver could do worse than serve an apprenticeship with the Great Northern Railway at Doncaster. One of Lee's parishioners was none other than Henry A. Ivatt, who had taken over as Locomotive Superintendent in 1895, following the death in service of his predecessor, Patrick Stirling. Ivatt had been apprenticed at Crewe under Francis Webb, and after various moves, joined the GS&WR, in due course becoming Chief Mechanical Engineer at Inchicore in 1886. Ivatt was persuaded to interview Bulleid, and was impressed enough to offer him a premium apprenticeship. Bulleid proved to be a keen pupil, and on completion of his apprenticeship in 1906, was appointed personal assistant to the Locomotive Running Superintendent. He became personal assistant to the Works Manager in the following year. Two years before this, the GNR had appointed Herbert Nigel Gresley to the position of Carriage & Wagon Superintendent at Doncaster.

Bulleid made his mark in other ways. In July 1901, he was invited to tea with the Ivatt family, and before long, he had fallen in love with the youngest daughter, Marjorie, whom he married on 18th November 1908. Later that year, he went to work for the French branch of Westinghouse, but only three years later, he decided that it was time to return to Britain. Ivatt had retired in the autumn of 1911, so Bulleid persuaded Gresley, who was now in charge, to take him back at Doncaster, where he became Gresley's personal assistant. He was to remain with the GNR and London & North Eastern Railway for the next twenty-six years, apart from a spell in France during the Great War. It is interesting to note that no Bulleid influence was to be found in the locomotive history of the L&NER. That said, Bulleid is reputed to have referred to the wedge-shaped front-end of the A4 class as Bugatti's and the aerofoil over the wheels as his. Perhaps Gresley had already seen some inkling of Bulleid's unorthodox ideas!

Move to the Southern

In any event, Richard Maunsell, CME of the Southern Railway since 1913, and a one-time pupil of Ivatt at Inchicore, announced his retirement on 28th May 1937. Bulleid was approached by Sir Herbert Walker, General Manager of the Southern, and persuaded to seek an interview. The result appears to have been a foregone conclusion, and Bulleid took up residence at Waterloo on 20th September 1937. Little need be said of Bulleid's Pacifics or the Q1 0-6-0s, which have been described in other publications. Three items of particular note, however, apart from their unconventional and even ugly appearance, might be mentioned, the extensive use of welding, the unique chain driven motion, and their superb boilers.

The most unusual of all the Bulleid designs, and the one closest in many respects to his Turf Burner on CIE, was the Leader. The first ideas for a radical new design of engine dated back to 1944, when the question of a replacement for the M7 0-4-4Ts was raised by the traffic manager. Some mention was made of a large tank engine, but Bulleid was of opinion that twenty-five more Q1s should be constructed. In March 1945, drawings for what was basically a Q1 design were prepared, but with the air-smoothed casings of the Pacifics (Bulleid never referred to these engines as being streamlined). Later, the idea of a type of tank engine with multiple cylinders on two six-wheeled bogies was put forward. This engine still bore a strong resemblance to the Merchant Navy class in outward appearance. Here the resemblance ceased, for beneath the casing new ideas were forming, including the notion of a firebox in which only the crown was covered by water, and cylinders with sleeve valves.

With the Brighton drawing office producing more and more drawings to order, it was obvious that some form of

Another view of a Bulleid Pacific, this time Battle of Britain class No 34089 "602 Squadron" working hard as she passes Bickley on the down Ostend Boat Train in April 1958. This photograph is included to show the problems associated with steam and smoke drifting down across the cab, even with smoke deflectors fitted. The fitting of deflectors to CC1 did help in some measure.

testbed would be required. In consequence, class H1 Atlantic No 2037 "Hartland Point" was chosen to be the "guinea pig". New cylinders with sleeve valves were fitted, and for ease of access the running plate was cut away behind the cylinders. In addition, a new stovepipe double chimney was fitted and in general what had been a neat design became ugly. In the meantime, work had been proceeding on the prototype and Leader was reported to be ready for trials on 21st June 1949. The final design was for a boiler, fuel bunker and water tanks enclosed within a framed sheet steel casing to form the fireman's cab in the middle, with a driving cab at each end. All three cabs were interconnected by a narrow corridor down one side, the boiler being offset 6in from its centre line to accommodate this. Was this an idea borrowed from Gresley's corridor tenders?

Extensive use was made of welding. Two six-wheeled power bogies were provided, each with three 12¼in x15in cylinders with sleeve valves. Final drive was the same chain-driven variant of Walschaerts valve gear as in the Mer-

chant Navy class. The centre crank axle of each bogie was fitted with a sprocket on each side, chains leading thence to the inner and outer axles. This unsymmetrical drive was to cause problems with unbalanced stresses on the crank axle, and might have been the cause of a broken crank axle whilst on a trial run from Eastleigh on 29th June 1950. On the other hand, flaws were found in the second bogie, pointing perhaps to a possible design fault.

The details of the various test runs need not concern us here. However, it is worth mentioning that of some seventy runs made from Brighton between June 1949 and February 1950, a total of thirty-three, or just over 47%, were classed as failures. There were many reasons for these failures, the principal one being the all-too-frequent breakages of the sleeve valves. The firebox was lined with cast-iron firebricks, which were prone to fall out of position. This became more and more of a problem as the dry firebox sides distorted. Later, 9in wide firebricks were substituted, effectively reducing the grate area from 43 to 25½sq.ft, this latter figure

Q1 0-6-0 No C8, a 'Utility' type, designed by Bulleid during the War years. Note the patent Bulleid Boxpok wheels, lack of running plate and generally ugly appearance. Bulleid initially used his (then) novel numbering system on all his early locomotives. C8 was photographed at Feltham in March 1950.

being only about 25% greater than a CIE 101 class with the superheated Z boiler. Control of the regulator and the reverser were reported to be erratic, the latter being difficult to notch up. Minor irritants included a reluctance on occasions to reverse and difficulty in watering due to the height of the filler above water columns. On the plus side, the boiler was never washed out, and tube cleaning was rarely performed.

The total cost of the Leader project was quoted as £178,865; of this figure no less than £131,600 was expended on numbers 36002-5, none of which was completed. In a report commissioned early in 1950 by Robert Riddles, CME of British Railways, R.G. Jarvis, chief draughtsman at Brighton Works, commented that "the disappointing progress made with the locomotive to date is to a much greater extent attributable to the detail design than to the broad conception". Bulleid submitted a report in March 1950, in part saying, "I shall

always appreciate deeply having been permitted to follow the development of the Leader engine so far, as it has given me much valuable information for future work". Clearly this was a reference to his work with CIE. The final story in the chapter of the Leader came in a report from Riddles in November 1950 when he recommended the scrapping of the five engines. No public announcement was made and the engines were quietly cut up. Kevin Robertson in his history of Leader states that when Riddles gave the order for work to stop on numbers 36002-5, some officials from CIE travelled to Brighton with a view to purchasing the incomplete locomotives. Whilst there is no confirmation of this here, it is quite possible that such a visit was made. We have, however, moved rather ahead chronologically, and must now return to Ireland and the year 1948.

In 1952, British Railways embarked on a series of trials on various types of steam locomotive at what was then the newly equipped locomotive testing plant at Rugby. Such a plant had been planned for many years but there had been a reluctance by the 'Big Four' companies before nationalisation to contribute towards it. Accordingly the facility was only opened at a time when steam was in decline, and the lessons such a facility could provide in so far as improved efficiency, were never totally developed. Only one Bulleid type was ever tested at Rugby, Merchant Navy 4-6-2 No 35022 "Holland America Line" and this proved the superb capacity of the Bulleid boiler, which was never fully extended at the test plant, notwithstanding the fact that two firemen were employed.

One of the reasons for this was oil dripping from the oil bath onto the test rollers, which would then cause the locomotive to slip violently when 'at speed'. In normal working, any oil so deposited would have been left far behind on the track, so would not have been a problem. At the time, John Click was working as an engineer at Rugby and would later be seconded to the CIE as assistant to Bulleid. Click had already gained a wealth of experience of the way Bulleid's design concepts were developing at Eastleigh with Leader and proved to be a valued supporter of CC1 at Inchicore.

6

THE MILNE REPORT

In July 1948, the Minister for Industry and Commerce, Daniel Morrisey, wrote to Sir James Milne, former general manager of the GWR, asking him to undertake a review of rail, road and canal transport in the Republic. Apart from his three principal assistants, three further 'technical assessors' were put at his disposal by the British Transport Commission. These included O.V.S. Bulleid, at the time still Chief Mechanical Engineer of the Southern Region of the recently nationalised British Railways. The report, which was wide ranging, was submitted to Government early in December 1948. As far as this book is concerned, we are only interested in the sections dealing with locomotives and the organisation of responsibilities at Inchicore, the principal locomotive, carriage and wagon works on CIE. Bulleid's hand can be clearly seen in certain aspects of the report, and we will now deal with the relevant sections.

As has already been referred to, CIE had turned its attention to the wholesale dieselisation of the system. When consideration was being given to this matter, General Motors Corporation (Electro Motive Division) of La Grange, Illinois, as early as May 1947, offered their services, one of the suggestions being a Type EX locomotive as illustrated in Appendix M. Considerable correspondence ensued, right up to September 1952, in the course of which it became clear that GM would not supply completed locomotives, but expected CIE to carry out work at Inchicore. In any event, the whole scheme faltered when the Government refused to make available the necessary dollars for the purchase. In the interim, CIE had placed orders for five diesel shunting locomotives, two 915hp freight locomotives and six 1,830hp passenger/freight locomotives, to be built at Inchicore, with the intention of commencing with the adoption of diesel traction on a large scale. The large locomotives were to be each powered by two of the 915bhp Sulzer engines. Bulleid thought it unwise to presume from the information then available that this form of traction would prove to be the most suitable for requirements in Ireland, or whether their use could be justified economically.

The 915hp units were due for delivery in November 1948, but as regards the six big locomotives, it was considered that their use was unwarranted, and it was recommended that every endeavour be made to cancel the order. It was in due course necessary to take delivery of the twelve 915hp diesel engines; these were later used in the BRCW built B class A1A-A1A locomotives introduced by CIE in 1956. It was thought that there was considerable scope for diesel railcars as they would be capable of operating light loads at less cost than steam locomotives. The report recommended that, "an order be placed, for experimental purposes, for the purchase of a limited number of cars to work both as single units and as train sets, somewhat similar to those being acquired by the GNR(I)". This was an unusual suggestion at that time as

the GNR(I) 600 class railcars had not then been ordered, although it is possible that some preliminary discussions had taken place with manufacturers; it hardly referred to railcars F and G, then in use on the Northern system. Later, sixty railcars were purchased from AEC, similar to the GNR(I) 600 class railcars, with a further six being built at Inchicore with Bulleid designed bodies.

The Boiler Order is Cancelled

It will be recalled that reference has been made to the condition, etc of boilers in the CIE fleet. Paragraph 121 of the Milne report stated that there were at the time considerable arrears of boiler repairs arising from a strike of workshop staff in 1947, and also the re-conversion of locomotives from oil to coal-burning. Deviating briefly from the Milne Report, a meeting chaired by the General Manager was held at Kingsbridge early in October 1948 in regard to the possible cancellation of the order for 94 boilers. There was considerable discussion as to how the recommendation to purchase these had been arrived at. One of the difficulties had been that of obtaining steel, that procured from the USA having proved unsuitable for boiler work. Whilst raw materials could not be obtained, complete boilers could be supplied by British manufacturers. It was reported that the GNR(I) practice was to fit two new boilers in the life of an engine (approximately 47 years). Boilers were scrapped after two firebox lives and not on a mileage basis. It was normal to complete new boilers using all new materials, although occasionally old barrels and domes were used. Reference was made to a report prepared in 1929 by W.H. Morton (see Appendix B), when the economic life of a boiler was fixed at 550,000 miles or 22 to 23 years.

Obviously in reply to queries raised at this meeting, a lengthy memorandum was sent from Hinchcliffe to Lemass on 23rd October. In it he referred to the 'patch and mend' policy adopted during the emergency years that had led to the current situation. He did comment that while the whole matter had been constantly reviewed and discussed, no firm long-term policy had been adopted. He went on to say that the Morton report had been unknown to him and he had simply accepted the 550,000 miles formula as put forward by successive engineers since Morton's time. A copy of this memorandum had been sent to Tyndall, who also responded. On his appointment in May 1945, he found that the boiler position had been under consideration for some years, and also that some moves towards standardisation as recommended by Morton had been carried out. The building of new boilers at Inchicore was hampered by the non-availability of materials, the difficulty of obtaining experienced boilermakers, and now, the new diesel-electric locomotive programme.

If it was the intention to continue the 'patch and mend' method, the situation would soon be serious. Tyndall doubted whether this method was any more economical in the long term. A suggestion to build the timetable around the engine stock along the lines contemplated for diesels, thus reducing the existing stock of engines by 70 for an annual mileage of 9 million as against a pre-war figure of 12 million, would present quite a different picture that had not been considered when the new boilers were being ordered. The memorandum concluded by saying that if the present financial state of the company did not permit of this expenditure, the desired and looked for improvement in the output of the shops and the generally improved performance of locomotives "must be postponed again".

Two days before Hinchcliffe's memorandum was penned, the Government decision to cancel the order led to a telegram being sent to the Vulcan Foundry requesting that all work on the order should cease, and they confirmed that they had only ordered materials for the first 25 Z boilers. They wrote at the end of November 1948, stating that the actual costs involved, including loss of profit, amounted to £31,770. In view of the friendly relations existing between the two companies, and the fact that the cancellation did not rest entirely in CIE's hands, Vulcan were prepared to accept £25,000 in settlement. Having requested a breakdown of the £31,770, it became clear that £25,540 of this related to loss of profit, the balance representing materials delivered and a small account for dies and press tools for stampings. The large sum for loss of profit was immediately queried, Vulcan in reply pointing out that they had turned down requests to tender for approximately 60 boilers. Writing in April 1949, they advised that they had only managed to secure orders for 18 boilers.

The matter was now referred to legal advisers on both sides. Whilst initially the company declined to accept liability on the matter of loss of profits, their legal advisers subsequently advised that they would be required to prove conclusively that Vulcan had not suffered a loss. Vulcan's, "eminent London Counsel" were of the view that they were clearly entitled to compensation. Correspondence was now left to the legal teams to pursue. On enquiring of locomotive experts in Great Britain, it became clear that there had been a considerable slackening off in demand for locomotive work during 1949. Finally, in December 1949, a compromise settlement of £7,500 for loss of profits and £3,353 for materials and work done up to the date of cancellation was agreed.

Back to Milne

Details of the locomotive stock were given in the Milne Report. The total stock of broad-gauge engines as at 1st January 1948 was 461, of which 395 or 85.68% were over twenty-five years old, and no less than 102 were over sixty years in service. There were 65 classes of broad-gauge engines, of which 23 classes comprised only one engine. Even within classes, considerable variations occurred due to the use of different boiler types. Reference has already been made to the arrears of repairs. The mileage run between general repairs was in the region of 125,000 miles, a figure con-

siderably in excess of normal. On a typical day in August 1947, 138 of the total stock of 493 engines (broad and narrow gauge) were either under or were awaiting repairs. General repairs took an average of 151 days, other heavy repairs 64 and light repairs 22. These figures were very high compared with Britain.

Bulleid recommended that the number of engines should be reduced, as a first step, by 100, leaving a margin of 40 engines on peak days. A programme of breaking up should be based mainly on the withdrawal of classes in which there were fewest engines. He suggested 89 broad gauge engines in 31 classes, including the solitary 2-6-2T No 850 which had only been built in 1928. The maximum number of engines in any of these classes was eight. In view of the age of the present stock, and the desirability of standardisation, and limiting the number of types in service, it was recommended that a five year programme should be drawn up for the annual provision of ten new engines to be built at Inchicore, or elsewhere if necessary, and the reconstruction of a further ten each year. All new engines should be of a mixed traffic type, and full use should be made of this dual capacity. They should be designed as standard types to be perpetuated. It was probable that all traffic requirements could be met by three or four types of engine.

The last section of the Milne Report with which we need to concern ourselves was that headed 'Mechanical Engineering Department'. It was pointed out that the position of CME had been vacant since November 1944. Formerly, the CME had been responsible for the construction and maintenance of all railway rolling stock and locomotive operation. The Works Manager had taken over in November 1944 in a caretaker capacity, and after his death in May 1945, the Locomotive Running Superintendent was appointed to the dual post of Mechanical Engineer and Running Superintendent. Shortly afterwards, responsibility for the construction and maintenance of all carriage and wagon bodies was transferred to the Works Manager of the road vehicle body shop, leaving the carriage lifting shop at Inchicore in the charge of the Mechanical Engineer/Running Superintendent. In 1947, it was decided to transfer responsibility for the design of locomotives and rolling stock to the Road Chassis Production Manager, the Mechanical Engineer retaining responsibility for the locomotive erecting shops. It was clear that the work of the department was not being carried on efficiently, nor could it be. The report pointed out the urgent necessity for the appointment of a CME, who should be responsible for all mechanical and electrical engineering work.

Electricity Supply Board and Bórd na Móna

Following the foundation of the State, the Government decided to take a direct hand in the development of the national turf resources. The Turf Development Board, a private company financed by the State, was established in 1934. In the following year the new Board bought the Turraun Peat

Works, which had been set up by John Purser-Griffith near Ballycumber in Co. Offaly. For some years he had been successfully producing sod peat by mechanical means using German machinery adapted to Irish conditions.

In 1936 the Turf Development Board bought two undeveloped bogs of its own; a small one of 200 hectares at Lyrecrumpane, Co. Kerry, and a much larger one of 1,600 hectares at Clonsast, Co. Offaly. The Second World War delayed initial development, but much experience was gained which proved useful for later expansion. Turf produced during the War made a vital contribution to the nation's fuel supply at a time when imports of all kinds were severely restricted. A private company had set up a milling and briquetting plant at Lullymore, Co. Kildare, in 1933, but it got into financial difficulties some years later and eventually sold its bog and factory to the TDB.

By the end of the Second World War the Irish peat industry had proved itself, and plans were drawn up for an ambitious programme of expansion to exploit a much greater area of bogland. To carry out this task, the government decided to replace the Turf Development Board with a new organisation, and in 1946, Bórd na Móna (BnM) was set up by a special Act of the Oireachtas.

The Government's interest in the development of turf from the 1930s onwards had two main aims, firstly the development of as much native industry as possible, particularly in rural areas, and secondly the need for the nation to be as self-sufficient as possible in terms of energy resources. This second aim became a reality in the late 1940s, and through the 1950s with the rural electrification scheme implemented by the Electricity Supply Board (ESB). The ESB had been established in 1927 to co-ordinate the development of the national electricity generation and transmission network. They inherited the existing generating plants that had been established in the main cities, such as the old Pigeon House, which had been built for the Dublin Corporation Electricity Department in 1903. Two years prior to the establishment of the ESB, the Shannon Electricity Act had been passed, and work on the Shannon Hydro-electric Scheme commenced in September 1925, resulting in the State's first hydro-electric generating station at Ardnacrusha in Co. Limerick.

It was not until after the War that rural electrification on a nation wide basis was able to commence. In order to minimise dependence on imported fossil fuels, and to construct power plants at strategic points in the grid, the ESB decided to develop turf-fired generating stations supplied with fuel by BnM. The development of the turf-burning stations presented a considerable challenge to ESB engineers for this fuel, with its high moisture content, posed combustion problems that had to be solved. Their success can be measured by the fact that seven turf-fired generating stations were commissioned between 1950 and 1965, as seen in the table below.

By the end of the 1960s, approximately one-third of the ESB's total capacity was based on turf; of this two-thirds used milled peat and one-third sod peat. The fuel was transported in special narrow gauge trains operated by BnM, and in this respect it is interesting to note that the first purpose-built turf-fired steam locomotives were used in the transport of the fuel to Portarlington generating station from late 1949 onwards, further referred to below. It was this success in the use of turf as an indigenous fuel that led to the approval by the government of CIE's proposals to develop a turf-fired locomotive, at the same time opening the door for Bulleid to apply his extravagant ideas for improving the steam locomotive.

Three 0-4-0WT locomotives came from Andrew Barclay's works (Works numbers 2263-5) in 1949, and were numbered 1 to 3 by BnM. They were conventional steam locomotives, the only concessions to burning turf being their large spark arresting chimneys and their fireboxes, which were amply proportioned. Numbers 1 to 3 proved to be too heavy for running on the bog system, and saw little service with BnM, although they were reported to be successful as turf-burners. Happily, all three still exist today. Number 1 was sold in 1969 to the Talyllyn Railway in Wales, and has been rebuilt as a coal-fired, 2ft 3in gauge 0-4-2WT, numbered 7, and initially named "Irish Pete", later altered to "Tom Rolt". Number 2 is preserved by the Irish Steam Preservation Society Railway at Stradbally, Co. Laois, and is run on most Bank Holiday weekends, while number 3 went to Shane's Castle, Co. Antrim, where she was appropriately named "Shane". Number 3 is currently out of service.

Station	Location	Fuel	Opened	Capacity
Portarlington	Co. Laois	Sod peat	1950	37.5 MW
Allenwood	Co. Kildare	Sod peat	1952	40 MW
Ferbane	Co. Offaly	Milled peat	1957/61	60 MW + 30 MW
Lanesborough	Co. Longford	Sod and milled peat	1958/66	20 MW + 40 MW
Rhode	Co. Offaly	Milled peat	1960/63	40 MW + 40 MW
Bellacorrick	Co. Mayo	Milled peat	1963	40 MW
Shannonbridge	Co. Westmeath	Milled peat	1965/82	40 MW + 45 MW

BULLEID AND THE TURF BURNER

B2 class 4-6-0 No 405 at Cork. A diagram of the K boiler, as fitted to this class, was sent to Franco-Crosti. Did Bulleid have ideas of fitting a Crosti boiler to one or more of the class?

(H. Fayle, IRRS collection)

BR 9F 2-10-0 No 92028 at an open day at Derby in September 1955, fitted with a Franco-Crosti boiler. In the case of the 9Fs, the preheaters were arranged below the boilers giving the members of the class so fitted a massive appearance.

7

BULLEID COMES TO INCHICORE

Bulleid returned to England following his duties on the Milne Report, and in due course resigned his position as CME, Southern Region of BR as from September 1949. The story goes that he had made an impression on Thaddeus C. Courtney, who had become Chairman of CIE in February 1949, and he was invited by the latter to become Consulting Mechanical Engineer, succeeding to the vacant post of Chief Mechanical Engineer a year later. In an interview shortly after Bulleid's appointment in 1949, he stated his interest in developing the use of turf as a locomotive fuel.

As early as April 1950 J.J. (Jackie) Johnston, by now the Assistant Chief Mechanical Engineer, had written requesting authority to purchase some equipment, "in connection with experimental work at present in hand for the burn-

ing of turf in steam locomotives". BnM were also involved at this early stage, having loaned CIE a sod breaker. Bulleid, writing to BnM in September 1950, confirmed that a number of experiments had been carried out into the burning of machine-won and milled turf in confined spaces. These tests ranged from comparatively small laboratory experiments up to tests carried out on stationary boilers to ascertain the ratio between the steam output of locomotive boilers when using turf and coal. Bulleid was able to confirm that using machine-won turf in a pressurised grate working on a two stage air injection principle produced steam outputs equivalent to, and in some cases in excess of, those normally obtained by the use of coal. Milled turf had been used in suspension in the combustion chamber of one of the Inchicore Power House boil-

Side view of boiler and cab of No 356 in the Erecting Shop at Inchicore during construction.

(Anthony O'Toole)

No 356 in the works at Inchicore. Some attention is clearly being focussed on one of the Crosti pre-heaters, seen here in their original, circular form. The lack of a chimney will be noted.

(Anthony O'Toole)

ers. The overall view of the tests to date indicated that they were worth following up.

In reply to a Parliamentary question in October 1950, regarding the development of a turf-burning locomotive, Bulleid commented that the problem was complicated by the necessity to proceed on two lines of development, namely the use of turf in existing locomotives and the design of a new locomotive. Howden, who had become General Manager of CIE in 1950, replied to the Department of Industry & Commerce to the effect that the CIE board was not prepared at that stage to make any observations on progress to date. A similar response was given in February 1951. The first indications that experiments were about to be carried out with a locomotive came in the following month, with the order of a stoker engine from Beyer Peacock & Co at a cost of £374. The locomotive chosen for these trials was K3 class 2-6-0 No 356, which had been supplied new to the GS&WR as an 0-6-0 in 1903 by the North British Locomotive Co (Works No 15944). Owing to difficulties in negotiating sharp curves and excessive weight on the leading coupled wheels, she was rebuilt by the GS&WR as a 2-6-0.

By October 1951, a new tender was in course of construction for No 356, while the Foundry was occupied in casting a new grate. At that stage, although there was still a considerable amount of work to be done, it was confidently hoped to have the engine ready by the end of the year. This aspiration proved to be optimistic. Writing to Frank Lemass in mid-January 1952, Bulleid commented that provision would have to be made for fuelling at Thurles, and requested that a turf macerator be purchased from Denmark at a cost of £413. He was informed that he should carry on for a period by having the turf macerated at Inchicore and despatched in

wagons to Thurles. Permission was also sought, and granted, for the appointment of Séan Heneghan as Technical Assistant to supervise the trial runs. In reply to an enquiry in March, Bulleid reported that the expenditure to date totalled £3,221 for the necessary work on No 356 and £2,745 for the provision of the new tender. Of the total of £5,966, approximately £4,550 related to wages, the balance to materials. In addition, £5,078 had been expended on the preliminary experiments with stationary boilers. A year later the total had reached £15,738.

The principal modifications to No 356 were to the firebox and the provision of the new tender. The firebox was fitted with tuyères running front to back like conventional firebars. These were upturned U-shaped firebars with 1 inch diameter holes, numbering approximately fifty to each tuyère (pronounced 'twyer'). They were spaced about 4 to 5 inches apart, the intervening gap being filled with turf. In the initial stages with the pressurised firebox (referred to below), air was forced up between the tuyères from underneath, whereas the induced draft came from above. The firebox was fitted with a conventional brick arch.

It would appear that Bulleid had, at an early stage, made contact with the Italian firm of Locomotive A Vapore Franco, regarding the possible use of a Crosti boiler. At this point in our narrative, a brief description of the Franco-Crosti boiler might not go amiss. During 1939, Attilio Franco and Dr. Piero Crosti, two engineers of the Ferrovie dello Stato (FS) modified a Gr671 with pre-heaters on each side of the boiler; this locomotive was reclassed Gr672 and numbered 001. The purpose of this modification was to make better use of heat remaining in the exhaust gases. The firebox gases went through the normal boiler and then through the pre-

BULLEID COMES TO INCHICORE

heater, which heated the feedwater before it reached the boiler. Feedwater was delivered to the pre-heater at full boiler pressure and then passed directly into the main boiler through clack valves. To further increase efficiency, the exhaust steam heated a jacket around the outside of the pre-heater. It was central to the project that the pre-heater did not boil the water, but remained at a substantially lower temperature than the boiler, so it could absorb heat from combustion gases cooled thereby.

As out shopped, No 356 certainly had circular Crosti type pre-heaters down each side of the boiler. Later, following a visit to Italy, Bulleid called for an altered design, Séan Heneghan designing the oval pre-heaters with which the locomotive later ran. These were made of aluminium and were prone to steam leaks. At this stage however, construction of the prototype was under way and no further modifications were made. It is interesting to record that British Railways fitted up ten of their 9F 2-10-0s with Franco-Crosti boilers about this time. Instead of passing hot gases out through the chimney, they were turned 180° and passed through a tubular heat exchanger, before being ejected through a chimney just in front of the cab on the fireman's side. The heat exchangers on the 9Fs were located below the boiler, giving the locomotives a very massive appearance, whereas they were placed on either side of the boiler on No 356.

No 356 was initially reported to be a very difficult locomotive to steam. There was no way of regulating turf input to the firebox, which was fed by means of a worm screw and a forced draft (described in some correspondence as a pressurised firebox). There was no firehole door, only a small porthole about 6in by 4in as an inspection hatch. This hatch soon became covered in a tarry substance and it was therefore

very difficult to see the fire. Turf tended to back up at the rear of the firebox, and the fire would virtually go out. This was a vicious circle as a drop in boiler pressure compounded the situation. When the fire re-ignited, pockets of carbon monoxide and other volatile gases in the ducting were ignited, causing violent explosions. After a while, the regular operatives were able to produce these explosions at will, which were on occasions induced to discourage unwelcome guests. On one such occasion, Bulleid turned up unannounced but he was apparently oblivious to the pyrotechnics laid on. When leaving the footplate however, he turned to the late Norman Binns and said to him, "Binns, that could be dangerous"!

Initially, the evaporation rate was poor due to the difficulties in burning the turf. Séan Heneghan came up with the idea of an induced draught, and mentioned it to the Chief Draughtsman, Paddy Mulvany. In due course, Heneghan was called up before Bulleid to explain his ideas. He suggested to Bulleid that a bus engine would probably suffice to drive the necessary fan. Immediately, Bulleid picked up the telephone and called the Broadstone, and said he was sending Heneghan over to collect such an engine. This was in due course mounted on a flat wagon hauled behind the tender. After this, there was no difficulty in controlling the air input and the evaporation rate increased by some 60%. The only difficulty with the bus engine was the controlling of the throttle. Correspondence with Messrs Ricardo Consulting Engineers confirms that this system was in use by March 1953 and was giving good results.

No 356 was fitted with hot water injectors. These were necessary due to the pre-heating of the water. However, problems were encountered when the water level in the tender tank dropped. The input of steam from the pre-heaters

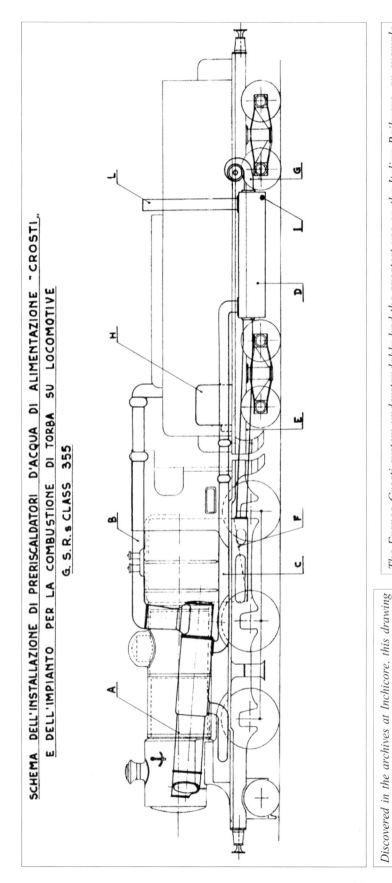

SCHEMA DELL'INSTALLAZIONE DI PRERISCALDATORI D'ACQUA DI ALIMENTAZIONE "CROSTI,

E DELL'IMPIANTO PER LA COMBUSTIONE DI TORBA SU LOCOMOTIVE

G. S. R. s CLASS 355

The Franco-Crosti system understandably had the greatest use on the Italian Railways, an example of this being with the GR 743 type of 2-8-0, 94 of which were built from 1940. A number also had a streamlining. Without the streamlined casing, however, the similarity to No 356 is apparent, with pre-heaters either side and no chimney on the smokebox. One example is preserved.

Discovered in the archives at Inchicore, this drawing was clearly produced by the Italian firm of Locomotive a Vapore Franco regarding the possible use of a Crosti boiler on No 356 - the proposed bogie tender will be noted. Perhaps typically, Bulleid was to modify the design - his assertion being that to use peat and not coal negated the patent. This did not, though, prevent the Societa Franco-Crosti of Milan, approaching the CIE General Manager. F. Lemass, through the Italian Minister in relation to patent rights in 1954, a figure of £900 being suggested. The letter was passed to the CIE Solicitor, Brendan A. McGrath whose report appears to attempt to distance CIE from Bulleid somewhat, on the basis that the designer appeared to have met the Italians on a personal rather than formal basis. Accordingly, McGrath's advice was a carefully worded reply; "We were interested in the device and did carry out some experiments, which proved unsuccessful...". After this matters appear to have rested, although whether the decision to later physically modify the shape of the pre-heaters was affected by the patent position is not clear. The letters on the drawing refer to a key which has not been located.
(CIE, IRRS collection)

No 356. View taken from ground level looking forward from the cab and clearly showing the left-hand pre-heater and associated ducting.

(Anthony O'Toole)

Above:
No 356 with the access doors removed from the smokebox and one of the Crosti-type pre-heaters clearly showing the tube arrangement. Not visible is that the access doors were secured by a circular wheel mounted at the centre of each, as seen on the views of the pre-heaters on page 41.

Left:
Rear view of tender on No 356.

(Both, Anthony O'Toole)

Cab view of No 356 show-
ing the turf feed arrangements from the tender to the
firebox. Although not obvious from this photograph,
No 356 did not, as rebuilt,
have a conventional firebox
door. Instead a small in-
spection window was pro-
vided although in practice
this was quickly obscured
by tar-like deposits.

(Anthony O'Toole)

Top left: View from the rear of the tender showing details of the turf hoppers. (Anthony O'Toole)

Top right: The turf feed on No 356. Difficulties were encountered with the ingestion of rags and other foreign material, it being suspected that these had sometimes been deliberately introduced. (Anthony O'Toole)

Left: No 356 in the Erecting Shop. Whilst not of the best quality, this is the only view to clearly show the Leyland bus engine on the wagon behind the tender, later provided to assist in the drafting. The overall length of the completed engine, tender, and wagon can thus be gauged. 2nd September 1953. (M. Bland)

Above:

No 356 being fuelled at Inchicore. The person standing on the right on top of the tender is believed to be Séan Heneghan, the technical assistant in charge of road trials.

(Anthony O'Toole)

Right:

A good view of the rear of No 356's tender showing the pre-heating ducts. Also visible are the access doors which proved to be too small when a fitter endeavoured to replace a turbine at Mallow as referred to in the text.

(Anthony O'Toole)

BULLEID AND THE TURF BURNER

No 356 during early steaming trials at Inchicore. On the left-hand side can be seen the equipment for supplying turf to the tender.

(Anthony O'Toole)

was constant and the lesser volume of water became hotter. This problem was to lead to some anxious moments when the injectors refused to lift. The problem was cured by substituting a Weir pump; a similar pump was later used on the prototype locomotive.

Turf was supplied from Clonsast as ovals about the size of tennis balls, although these tended to break up on their passage through the worm drive. The lower photograph on page 39, however, appears to suggest that larger pieces of turf were subsequently provided. One of the problems encountered with the worm was the ingestion of rags, even though the turf was carefully screened before use. It is possible that in some cases, these rags may have been maliciously introduced to sabotage experiments. The rags wound themselves round the worm, bringing it to a sudden stop and causing breakages. To overcome the problem of breakages, shear

bolts were installed. The turf ash remained alive for a long time even with careful dousing with water, and was prone to blow around more than coal ash. Every time a lineside fire occurred, even though No 356 had not been out on trial, she was blamed. She was fitted with spark arrestors, but they were not entirely satisfactory in coping with the fine turf ash.

A number of test runs were made out on the mainline, generally to Kildare, with water being taken at Sallins and Kildare. The regular crew consisted of Driver Jim Brady and Fireman John Ryan. Both were excellent enginemen, Ryan being very proficient at handling the hot water injectors, while Brady was described as being a super driver who was quite unflappable. Heneghan relates a story that on one occasion Bulleid called for an unscheduled trial. Norman Binns, from the Drawing Office, who was normally out on such trials, was on holiday, so Heneghan agreed to take out

BULLEID COMES TO INCHICORE

No 356 at Inchicore, leaking steam from almost every conceivable position.

(Anthony O'Toole)

No 356 in steam at Inchicore. On the right are several wagons of turf briquettes awaiting transfer to No 356's tender. The driver is believed to be Jim Brady, the regular driver during the trials.

(Anthony O'Toole)

BULLEID AND THE TURF BURNER

An interesting view of No 356 outside Inchicore Works with the down Belfast-Dublin-Cork Enterprise express passing, in charge of B2 4-6-0 No 407.

(Anthony O'Toole)

the engine. Both Brady and Ryan were also absent on that day, and he was given a crew who were less than enthusiastic. In fact the driver was by nature a nervous individual, and was reportedly terrified of the engine. In due course, the fire blacked out at Sallins, and the fireman was unable to get the injectors to work. Séan Heneghan did all he knew to revive the fire and coax the injectors to work, but in time the inevitable happened – a violent explosion occurred and blew the flexible bellows off the top of the cab. On looking round, Heneghan discovered that he was alone on the footplate and it took some persuasion to get the two men back on board.

Some time ago, a letter appeared in the *Railway Magazine* under the title 'Revealed – secrets of the turf burner's implosion', in which the writer referred to an incident involving the tender of No 356 which was reported to have imploded. This so-called incident appears to have been the figment of a young apprentice's imagination, or else he was set up in true Inchicore fashion. The present author drew the attention of Séan Heneghan to the letter in question, and he could only conclude that the Sallins incident referred to above had become much embellished over the years. He had certainly never come across this occurrence, and one would have expected him to have at least heard of it since he was so closely involved with No 356. It would seem that the distortion occurred to the story, not to No 356's tender. Apart from anything else, the tender was not under any pressure, at very worst the water would have approached boiling point, and

there were a number of access points which would have permitted any unlikely build-up of pressure to escape harmlessly to the atmosphere.

A trial run was made to Cork on 9th June 1953 with a load of 521 tons behind the tender, a banking engine being provided as far as Clondalkin. The locomotive steamed very satisfactorily on this run, with improvements on goods running times over a number of sections. Steam was actually blowing off on the climb of Ballybrophy bank. Between Mallow and Cork, however, steaming was poor due to an air leak on the sheet metal pipe to the induction fan on the truck behind the tender. After a temporary repair had been effected, matters improved. Details of this run are set out in Appendix G.

Heneghan tells another amusing anecdote about this run. Both he and Norman Binns were on the footplate and they had been booked in to the Imperial Hotel in Cork for the night. The train did not arrive in Cork until 22.30 and it was nearly midnight by the time the engine had been disposed of. The two men considered whether they should go to the Imperial Hotel at that hour of the night, particularly as they were extremely dirty following a long day on the footplate. Binns was a large man of about 18 stone, with bushy hair and a long handlebar moustache (he had in fact been in the Royal Air Force) and seemed to have a propensity for attracting dirt. The locomotive inspector in Cork suggested that they spend the night in the Enginemen's dormitory, which they decided

K3 2-6-0 No 356 in steam outside the Works at Inchicore. At this stage, No 356 was not equipped with a chimney, nor did she have the trailing wagon with the internal combustion engine.

(Anthony O'Toole)

to do. This latter was run by a lady, who on seeing the pair on the doorstep screamed and disappeared. It took some time and persuasion for them to effect an entry. One can only imagine the reception they would have received at the Imperial!

No 356 was turned in Cork, it being necessary to separate the wagon with the diesel engine to effect this, and set out on the return journey. The engine failed however at Mallow when a rotor ring on the turbine came adrift. The engine remained in Mallow for about two weeks until a replacement turbine was sent down. When a boilermaker came up from Cork to replace the unit, he discovered that the door through which it had apparently been installed was too small, a new piece having been welded on following the installation of the turbine. It was clear from the efforts of the boilermaker that the removal of this was going to be a slow process, trying

severely the patience of Norman Binns. Séan Heneghan tells of Binns removing the offending plate by sheer brute force. After resuming the journey from Mallow, a wagon caught fire near Dundrum. The train was brought to a stand in Dundrum station, the station master calling out the fire brigade. Two wagons on the train were destroyed.

No 356 was painted in an aluminium livery and as such bore the following inscription on the tender:

C I E

Experimental Turf Burning Locomotive

There is a story told that it was not long before the 'Experi' part of the inscription was left obscured when the remainder of the tender was cleaned. It has not been possible to

In steam, and seemingly without any leaks this time. The additional casings necessary to house the various pipework detracted from the view that the crew had from the cab. *(Anthony O'Toole)*

authenticate this but it is quite within the bounds of possibility at Inchicore! Whilst No 356 provided much useful experience and test data, it could hardly be considered a success as a turf-burning locomotive. Some useful ideas were, however, to be incorporated in the prototype locomotive.

Consultants are appointed

In December 1951, Bulleid wrote to his old friend Sir Harry Ricardo of Ricardo & Co Ltd of Shoreham-by-Sea in West Sussex, seeking drawings showing the arrangement for oscillating a sleeve valve. Apart from Bulleid's earlier use of these valves in the Leader, their principal application was to be found in aero engines, a field in which Ricardo was an expert. The matter progressed a stage further in January 1952, when Bulleid stated a requirement for an engine, probably three-cylindered, and giving an output of 100 to 150 hp. At about this time, Ricardos were experimenting with a small steam engine intended to burn wood or any vegetable refuse. The engine in question had been designed in response to a request from the Indian Government for use on small farms,

to take the place of two buffaloes normally used for operating irrigation pumps and the like. Although of only 2 bhp continuous rating, the engine was of interest to Bulleid, as it used an aluminium casting, and being light, might therefore be suitable for use as a feed water heater. Some use of turf had been made, but the difficulty was in getting the lining of the firebox really hot with this fuel. Bulleid later offered to arrange for a quantity of turf briquettes to be sent over to Ricardos, who in turn actually enquired of Bulleid as to whether there might be a market for such an engine in Ireland, Bulleid passing the correspondence to Dr Andrews at BnM.

Writing in April 1952, Bulleid pointed out that he was using turbines to drive the fans on No 356, an extravagant way of doing so, and he enquired whether Ricardos might be able to supply two suitable engines. The idea did not appeal to the latter, who were of opinion that the cost of such limited production would be very high. In the following month, Bulleid raised the question of Ricardos acting as consultants in connection with the prototype Turf Burner, but it was not until the following October that Board approval was

No 356 outside Inchicore Works with plenty of steam visible. In this view, she has been fitted with a very ugly stovepipe chimney. This was used purely for lighting-up purposes.

(Anthony O'Toole)

obtained, the agreement to run for two years from 1st January 1953 at a fee of £500 per annum.

In June 1952 Bulleid advised Ricardos that the Morse Chain Co would not give any guarantee with their chains under the proposed application on the Turf Burner, which would therefore entail a look at the existing design. In reply, Sir Harry enquired, "Why on earth do you bother with Morse chains?" He thought the roller chain was far more suitable for high power transmission, and they had used it quite successfully for the final drive of 36-ton tanks in the 1914-18 War, their tractive effort being in the region of 40,000lb. In reply, Bulleid stated that he found it difficult to give an answer, except that the Morse chains had in his opinion worked perfectly satisfactorily on his Merchant Navy and West Country Pacifics. He also mentioned that he wondered whether he could obtain the drive required by means of Wiseman's resilient gears, so as to cut out chains altogether if possible. In

response to another of Bulleid's queries, Sir Harry replied simply, "My Dear Bulleid, after all these years have you not learnt? Ricardo."

By the following October, some further details were emerging. There were to be two six-cylinder single-acting engines with 9in by 9in cylinders, boiler pressure 250psi and 3ft 6in wheels, wheelbase 10ft and bogie centres 35ft. Starting tractive effort was to be of the order of 25,000lb. At this stage no decision had been made as to whether the engines would be mounted on the frame or in the bogies. An engine located on the mainframe would drive through a propellor shaft to a gearbox on the bogie, the power from the gearbox being transferred to the axles through subsidiary propeller shafts. Bogie mounting would, of course, simplify the question of the drive to the wheels. Ricardos now began work on a scheme for such an engine, reference being made to work done by their Mr Beard in connection with the BR Fell loco-

BULLEID AND THE TURF BURNER

No 356 outside Inchicore Works in her later guise. She has now been equipped with the oval pre-heaters down each side of the boiler and a modified ducting system over the top of the cab. Also to be noted is the trailing wagon with internal combustion engine (from a scrapped Leyland bus). Another modification is the sloping tray at the front end, presumably to assist in cleaning out the smokebox. The smokebox door itself clearly shows signs of burning, no doubt due to an accumulation of ash within.

(IRRS collection)

motive in relation to gearing. By January 1953, the preference appeared to be for frame mounted engines with a gear drive. Angular movement of the bogies was estimated at $3^5/_8$in each side of the longitudinal centre line; this would be too great for a direct chain drive, and a cardan shaft and bevel drive was being considered.

About this time, an interesting idea was being put forward by Bulleid aside from the turf burner project. The AEC railcars were now in service, and Bulleid referred to a proposed design for a "power van with four 11.3 litre (diesel) engines each driving one axle of the four axles on the two four-wheeled bogies". He felt that the same arrangement might be considered for four steam engines using as much of the gearing as possible. It is not stated in the correspondence exactly what these power vans were to be utilised for, but it can be assumed that they were to be some type of shunting locomotive. A Ricardo memorandum lists various points in relation to the turf-burning design. It was suggested that the same chassis and gear transmission as the AEC 'locomotives' be used, but that the centre engines be omitted (Bulleid had now opted for six axles, only four of the six axles being driven). Later, Bulleid decided on six AEC engines, later still with the four outer engines substituted by 150hp steam engines.

As regards the turf burner, a double-ended locomotive type boiler with a central firebox was to be used, the latter turf-fed from the side. Boiler pressure was again to be 250lb with a moderate degree of superheat. The steam engines were each to be of three vertical, short stroke (say 4¼in by 5in) cylinders. Though four speeds were unnecessary, it was deemed desirable to use the standard gearboxes as they were, possibly with alteration to the final drive gear ratio.

By this time, serious consideration was being given to the introduction of diesel-electric locomotives of not less than 1,000hp continuous rating, and as the turf-burning locomotive would be expected to take its place alongside, it would need to be at least as powerful. One of the designs being considered was the General Motors model 12LC-1, although as we know, only a few years previously the Government had quite unequivocally ruled out dollar spending. In answer to a query on general purpose diesel locomotives for CIE, Ricardos suggested that such locomotives should be fitted either with Daimler-Benz engines and a hydraulic transmission or two Breda engines with Sinclair couplings and 'Power Flow' gearboxes. As we know, against Bulleid's advice to buy American, preferably General Motors, the decision was made to obtain diesel-electric locomotives from Metropolitan Vickers of Manchester, fitted with Crossley engines, with disastrous consequences. It has to be said, however, that the introduction of these locomotives gave Inchicore a great insight into diesel locomotive practice and operation, which held them in good stead in the future. It is also ironic that after Bulleid's departure from Inchicore the decision was taken in 1960 to purchase the B121 class locomotives from General

BULLEID COMES TO INCHICORE

Metrovick / Crossley 1200hp Co-Co A class No A26 working a short freight train, and crossing the Crescent Bridge on Wexford Quays. A26 was in fact the last of the Metrovicks to receive a GM engine.

(David Lawrence / Hugh Davies)

Motors, arguably the best locomotives CIE ever had. Since then, all new locomotives have come from that source, and indeed the A and C classes were later re-engined with General Motors engines.

Reference has already been made to the pre-heating of the feed water. Ricardos suggested that a battery of the small aluminium boilers produced by them be used two abreast in several tiers to give the required heating surface. Some discussion ensued as to the number of these units required for the prototype. Inchicore suggested they would require 56, this figure being modified to 32. As there was an expectation of building fifty of these locomotives, it was suggested that the aluminium heaters should be constructed in the foundry at Inchicore.

Problems arose with the projected AEC locomotive when that firm advised that they had no gearboxes in production for the larger engine size, thus necessitating a return to the, "simple proposition of chain drive". At one point in March 1953, Bulleid stated that he had considered an electrical drive, but had rejected this on the grounds of cost. Bulleid was still considering the use of sleeve valves in May 1953. Ricardos expressed opposition to the use of these in steam locomotive practice, as cylinder distortion might well cause difficulties. In a letter to Bulleid, Sir Harry commented that he loved "the sleeve valve dearly, for it has so many virtues, but it must be treated with due respect". In the same letter, he suggested that conventional piston valves be employed, and went as far as suggesting a compound locomotive, "but here I hesitate, for I am treading on ground much better known to you than to me". Bulleid proposed lining the steel cylinder block with a ¼in cast-iron barrel to enable wear to be easily made good. Ricardos threw cold water on the notion of a steel

cylinder block in view of the widely different temperatures to be expected, varying from live steam temperature to that of exhaust steam. There could be a differential of as much as 400°F, which would cause excessive thermal distortion, and thus lead to major problems with the sleeve valves. Bulleid was of the opinion that distortion should not be a serious problem, but nevertheless turned his attentions to the possible use of piston valves.

In response to a question in Dáil Éireann on 19th November 1953 from Deputy MacBride concerning the progress being made with the development of a turf-fired locomotive by CIE, the Taoiseach (Prime Minister), Sean Lemass, brother of the CIE general manager, simply replied that work was proceeding, and that the CIE board had been made aware of his concern that the development should press ahead. Matters progressed, but Bulleid was beginning to show signs of frustration in March 1954. With the engine and transmission at a stage where tenders could be obtained for gears etc, it became clear that the cost and delivery times were problems that could not easily be overcome. As he was now coming under considerable pressure to produce a suitable engine at the earliest possible date, he had no option but to revert to steam locomotive practice. This decision was "arrived at with a great deal of reluctance and regret". With this setback, Ricardos saw no necessity for them to continue to act as consulting engineers, and the agreement was therefore terminated on 30th June 1954. It is of interest to note that some two years later, Bulleid enquired of them regarding the supercharging of the AEC railcar engines. Nothing further came of this idea. We will now revert to Inchicore and backtrack a little in time to look at the early proposals for the prototype locomotive.

45

Inchicore Works depicted in 1962. The Dublin to Cork main line runs just out of view on the extreme right, whilst various buildings are: A - Carriage Shop, B - Lifting Shop, C - Erecting Shop (later Diesel 1), D - Fabrication Shop, E - Inchicore Running Shed, F - Wagon Shop (later Diesel 2), G - Railcar Shed, H - Road Bus section. At the bottom is a row of company houses.

8

THE PROTOTYPE TAKES SHAPE

Whilst the various trials were taking place with No 356, plans were proceeding with the design of the prototype locomotive. A preliminary drawing dated 28th June 1951 shows a design for an 0-6-6-0 type, 68ft in length with turf and water capacities of 8½ tons and 2,700 gallons respectively. No further details are shown on the drawing except for the inclusion of a Howden air heater. Another, undated, drawing with a similar wheel arrangement indicates that turf and water would be carried at both ends. The only dimension on the drawing is for an air heater 6ft 3in long, which scaled up shows a length over body of 68½ft, presumably a development of the earlier design. By now, there appears to be an indication of the possible use of a Crosti type boiler with a water heater.

Two further drawings are of some interest. One, dated 24th July 1952 shows an 0-4-4-0, 50ft long, bogie centres 32ft, bogie wheelbase 8ft and driving wheels 3ft 8in. Turf and water were carried in two bunkers and tanks, each holding respectively 1.7 tons of turf and 1,000 gallons of water. These figures both indicate a restricted range between refuelling and watering stops. The second drawing, dated 1st September 1952, represents an 0-6-6-0 design, 50ft long, bogie centres 34ft 6in, bogie wheelbase 5ft 3in + 5ft 3in. Driving wheels were now 3ft diameter and height is shown as 13ft. Regrettably neither drawing shows cylinder arrangements.

It is worth mentioning here that two of Bulleid's acquaintances from British Railways were seconded through the kindness of Roland C. Bond, namely John Click and Ron Pocklington. There are few references to the latter, but his contribution to the design of the Turf Burner must be recorded. Click had joined the Southern Railway in late 1943 under Bulleid, becoming a draughtsman at Eastleigh, and later becoming Assistant Works Manager there. He was a dyed-in-the-wool steam man who had very set ideas and was a very forceful character. Stories are legion about him. He was apparently an individual who always wanted his own way. Whilst at Eastleigh, he periodically handed in his notice, the powers that be would capitulate and he would remain. It would appear that he later tried the same trick after he had moved to the locomotive testing plant at Rugby but his bluff was called and he left to take up teaching. He was given more or less free reign in the design and construction of the prototype at Inchicore. Click returned to England at the end of two years but maintained a connection with the locomotive right up to 1958.

Click was in many respects a kindred spirit to Bulleid, but could at times be quite antagonistic towards others. He appears to have resented interference or suggestions from any of his subordinates. Bulleid on the other hand was always prepared to listen to suggestions, no matter how fanciful they

might appear to be. Séan Heneghan informed the author that he was extremely apprehensive when he approached Bulleid regarding his idea for an induced draft. As we have already seen, Bulleid took the idea on board. Bulleid could also show a human side to his nature as witnessed by another of Séan's anecdotes. About the time he had a telephone first installed at home, there had been a spate of hot axle boxes on wagons. One very cold and frosty winter's night, he received a call from Bulleid directing him to go to the North Wall yard in Dublin and count the number of axle box covers missing on wagons departing on goods trains. Bulleid mentioned that a staff car was being sent around to collect him, and just as the conversation was coming to an end, he said, "Heneghan, I would hold on to the car if I were you, as it is going to be a very cold night and, by the way, there is a rug in the back".

Bulleid was also reported to be prolific at producing drawings or sketches of ideas going through his mind. He would frequently produce, say, six or eight sketches based on one idea, and it was wise to retain all of these and bring them to meetings as one never knew from day to day which variation was to be discussed. On one occasion, Paddy McLoughlin, the Works Manager, brought a number of such sketches home to study. Paddy had a large family and it was reported that, unknown to him, the children had got hold of the drawings and scribbled on them. He had the unenviable task of explaining the fact to Bulleid, who apparently accepted the explanation with good grace.

By March 1954, it was reported that the boiler of the prototype had been completed, and was expected to undergo early steam tests. The steel sections for the underframes, bogies and superstructure had been ordered, along with various ancillaries such as fans, feed pumps and safety valves. Bulleid wrote to Lemass in April pointing out that no specific

The completed boiler of CC1 awaiting installation.

BULLEID AND THE TURF BURNER

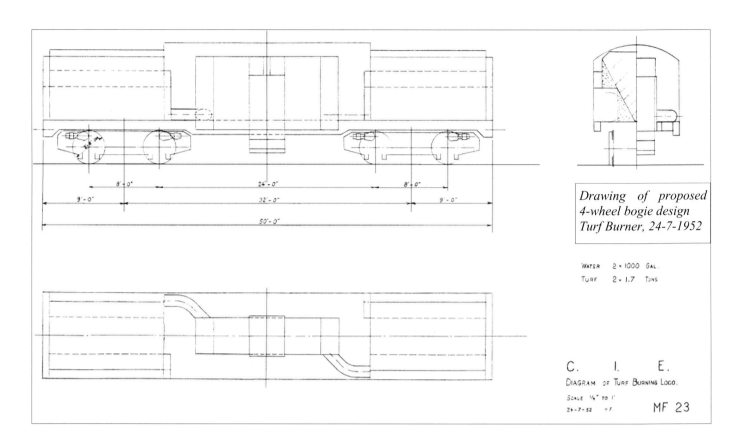

Drawing of proposed 4-wheel bogie design Turf Burner, 24-7-1952

WATER   2 × 1000 GAL.
TURF   2 × 1.7 TONS

C.   I.   E.
DIAGRAM OF TURF BURNING LOCO.
SCALE ¼" TO 1'
24-7-52   MF   MF 23

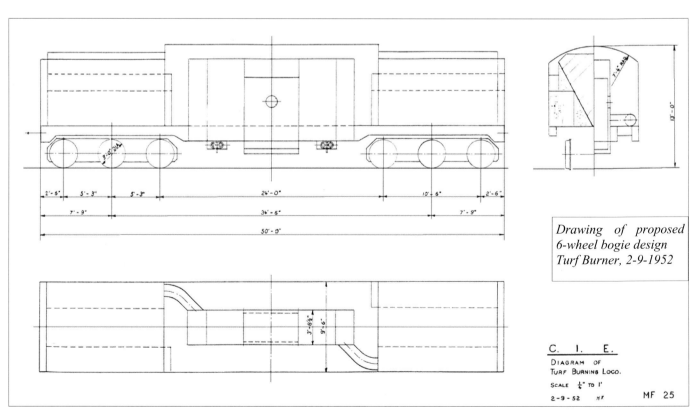

Drawing of proposed 6-wheel bogie design Turf Burner, 2-9-1952

C.   I.   E.
DIAGRAM OF
TURF BURNING LOCO.
SCALE ¼" TO 1'
2-9-52   MF   MF 25

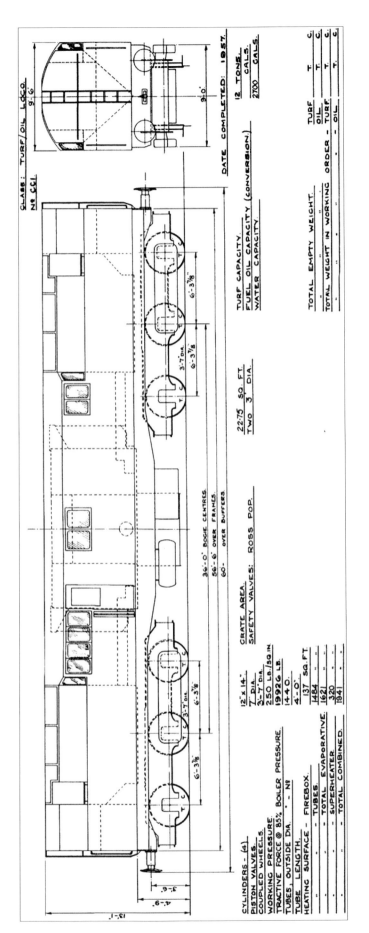

CLASS: TURF/OIL LOCO
Nº CC1

DATE COMPLETED: 1957.

9'-6"
9'-0"

TURF CAPACITY. .... 12 TONS.
FUEL OIL CAPACITY (CONVERSION). ...... GALS.
WATER CAPACITY. .... 2700 GALS.

TOTAL EMPTY WEIGHT. ...... TURF   T.   C.
                            OIL   T.   C.
TOTAL WEIGHT IN WORKING ORDER - TURF   T.   C.
                                 OIL   T.   C.

36'-0" BOGIE CENTRES.
56'-6" OVER FRAMES.
60'- OVER BUFFERS.

GRATE AREA. .... 22.75 SQ.FT
SAFETY VALVES: ROSS POP.   TWO 3" DIA.

6'-3⅛"   6'-3⅛"   3'-7" DIA.   6'-3⅛"   6'-3⅛"   3'-7" DIA.

CYLINDERS - (4) .... 12" x 14"
PISTON VALVES .... 7" DIA.
COUPLED WHEELS .... 3'-7" DIA.
WORKING PRESSURE .... 250 LB./SQ.IN
TRACTIVE FORCE @ 85% BOILER PRESSURE .... 19926 LB.
TUBES OUTSIDE DIA. - Nº .... 1440.
TUBE LENGTH. .... 4'-0.
HEATING SURFACE - FIREBOX. .... 137 SQ.FT
    ,,   ,,   - TUBES. 1484
    ,,   ,,   - TOTAL EVAPORATIVE. 1621
    ,,   ,,   - SUPERHEATER. 320
    ,,   ,,   - TOTAL COMBINED. 1941

3'-6"
4'-9"
13'-1"

Above: Weight diagram for the Turf Burner in its final form.

Left: Drawing of the precursor to Turf Burner - the SR "Leader". Apart from the obvious external similarities, the basic mechanical concept incorporated many similar ideas. In practice the final weight of "Leader" was far greater than that stated.

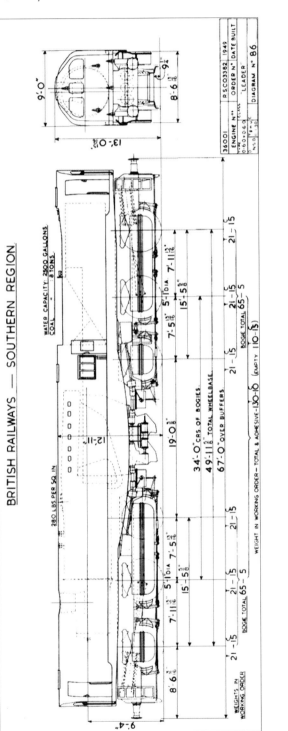

BRITISH RAILWAYS — SOUTHERN REGION

9'-0"
8'-6 9¼"
13'-0½"

WATER CAPACITY 2500 GALLONS
COAL 8 TONS
280 LBS PER SQ IN

8'-6⅜"   7'-11⅝"   7'-5⅝"   5'-10 DIA   15'-5⅝"   7'-5⅝"   7'-11⅝"   5'-10 DIA   15'-5⅝"
21-15   BOGIE TOTAL 65-5   21-15   21-15   BOGIE TOTAL 65-5   21-15

12'-11"
19'-0½"
34'-0" C'RS OF BOGIES
49'-11½" TOTAL WHEELBASE
67'-0" OVER BUFFERS

21-15   21-15   BOGIE TOTAL 110-(15)   21-15
WEIGHT IN WORKING ORDER - TOTAL & ADHESIVE 130-10 (EMPTY 130-10)

9'-4"

36001		PSCO3382 1949
ENGINE Nº	ORDER Nº	DATE BUILT
0-6-0+0-6-0	LEADER	DIAGRAM Nº 86

49

authorisation had been received from the Board for the construction of the Turf Burner, and such authority was now required by the stores superintendent. The reply from Lemass is of interest, "I think it is well established over the past four years that you have in hand the construction of a prototype turf-burning locomotive, and the Directors have authorised certain expenditure therefor. In the circumstances, I do not consider it necessary to secure specific Board authorisation at this date". Why, four years into the project was Bulleid expressing doubts?

Another interesting development occurred in April 1954, this time in relation to No 356. It will be recalled that some correspondence had passed between Locomotive A Vapore Franco and Bulleid in relation to the possible use of a Crosti-type boiler. Regrettably, Bulleid's own file is not available for perusal, but it would appear that Franco wrote seeking royalties on the Crosti patent. The correspondence was in due course submitted to the company solicitors, but even after nine months they had to admit that, "the problem is rather involved, and the information at my disposal is not sufficient to enable me to fully assess the exact legal position, despite a full perusal of the file of the Chief Mechanical Engineer". It was not until the end of January 1955 that a response was finally received from the solicitors' office. In the interim, the Italian Legation in Dublin had written to the company on behalf of Franco-Crosti.

As far as could be ascertained however, there was at no stage an express contract to pay for any services afforded to the Chief Mechanical Engineer by way of royalties or otherwise. However, there did appear to be strong grounds for a case on an implied contract for a payment in respect of technical advice and assistance. It was clear when Bulleid was formulating his ideas in 1951 that he was of opinion that the Franco-Crosti pre-heater would be suited to his requirements. It is also clear that he made early contact with the Ferrovie Dello Stato (Italian State Railways) who were at the time using the device. That early correspondence was passed to Locomotive A Vapore Franco and in due course Bulleid appears to have been supplied with plans. This was followed by meetings in Italy, Bulleid supplying Crosti with drawings of the 355 and 400 class locomotives with a request for information and data as to fitting them with the device. Was he thinking at that time of equipping one of the 400s for turf-burning or simply experimenting with steaming capacity?

The various meetings appear to have been on an informal basis, although drawings were in fact supplied by Crosti. Then, in a letter of January 1952, a reference was made to the payment of a royalty of £900 for each boiler constructed (CIE apparently intended to build the boilers themselves from drawings). The royalty was based on the value of coal saved in the first six months of operation with the pre-heater fitted. Bulleid countered the argument by stating that as he was experimenting with the use of turf this, "puts the application on a different footing". As far as the file of papers could be interpreted, no precise drawings of a Crosti boiler were supplied for either the 355 or 400 classes. The final conclusion was that some payment might be made. It is perhaps of interest to note that Roland Bond, in reference to the British Railways Crosti boilered 9F 2-10-0s, stated that the reduction in coal consumption was much less than had been predicted by the Crosti people, and as so often happened in the past, the saving in fuel costs was swallowed up by increased maintenance charges

As further testing continued, the Minister for Industry & Commerce sought information on how the work was proceeding and some idea of the possible date for completion of a prototype, along with the estimated cost of providing fifty locomotives. During the course of the next three years, evasive answers came from the CME's office. In fairness to Bulleid however, many modifications had to be made to improve efficiency. In December 1953, for example, he reported that a further experiment was being made to simplify the heat economiser by using aluminium ribbed drums in place of nests of smoke tubes. He also stated that the final drive to the bogie wheels would depend on the type of locomotive adopted in connection with the dieselisation programme, then in its early stages. It seemed desirable to use identical bogies under the diesel and turf-burning locomotives. Best

Opposite page, top:

Inchicore Works, Dublin, on 27th April 1957 with CC1 in course of construction. In the foreground is one of the locomotive's bogies, whilst behind is an E class Maybach shunter.

(N. Simmons / Hugh Davies)

Opposite page, bottom:

One of CC1's bogies, also on 27th April 1957. The 'BFB' Boxpok type wheel will be noted, as will the sprockets for the final chain drive. In this respect, the final drive was identical to the earlier Leader, with the chains running from centre to front on one side and centre to rear on the opposite side. Also clearly visible is the hand-brake wheel. Behind are two E class Maybach diesel-hydraulic shunting locomotives in the course of construction. To the right are an A class Metrovick/Crossley Co-Co (nearest the camera) and a B class BRCW/Sulzer A1A-A1A, both in original silver livery.

(Hugh Davies)

BULLEID AND THE TURF BURNER

CC1 No 1 end cab in the course of erection at Inchicore Works on the 23rd March 1957.

(G.F. Parrinder, G. Beesley collection)

CC1 No 2 hopper unit at Inchicore Works on 27th March 1957.

(G.F. Parrinder, G. Beesley collection)

THE PROTOTYPE TAKES SHAPE

CC1 No 1 end stoker in position in the mainframe on 21ˢᵗ March 1957.

(G.F. Parrinder, G. Beesley collection)

estimates indicated that the prototype might be available by the middle of 1955 at an estimated cost of £30,000.

This date proved to be optimistic, and in June of that year, Bulleid advised that the main and bogie frames for the prototype were complete, but delays in the delivery of steel were seriously hindering the completion of other components. In addition, work was being affected by a shortage of skilled draughtsmen and also by the dieselisation programme which was given priority, "over all other matters". This comment is interesting in the context of those who have in the past expressed the view that Bulleid spent a lot of time working on his plaything to the detriment of the dieselisation programme. Several letters from the Department for Industry & Commerce clearly indicate that political pressure to produce a locomotive capable of burning indigenous fuel was pushing the matter forward. This has also been confirmed by Click, who commented that the dieselisation programme, "resulting from a policy decision taken over his (Bulleid's) head, was also taking up a great deal of his time". It should be recalled that CIE had in the previous May placed an order with Metropoli-

tan Vickers of Manchester for the supply of sixty 1,200hp Co-Co and thirty-four 550hp Bo-Bo diesel electric locomotives (classes A and C respectively) with deliveries due to commence in June 1955.

The story of these locomotives does not directly concern us here, but suffice to say that steam remained in use on CIE rather longer than had been anticipated due to their considerable lack of reliability. Pilot engines were stationed at strategic points around the system for several years after their introduction and, as already stated, in course of time, they were rebuilt with General Motors engines. Meanwhile, work progressed slowly on the Turf Burner, there being considerable delays in the delivery of steel. A note of 9ᵗʰ February 1956, comments that Bulleid proposed to offer £5 per week expenses for British Transport Commission draughtsmen coming to Dublin for twelve months in connection with the project.

In response to yet another enquiry from the Minister of the Department for Industry & Commerce, Mr Norton, following further questions in the Dáil from Deputy MacBride

BULLEID AND THE TURF BURNER

CC1 feed screw and tube. Note the small clearance between the screw and the tube. Difficulties were encountered with this equipment on No 356 due to the ingestion of rags, believed by some to have been maliciously introduced to sabotage experiments.

(G.F. Parrinder, G. Beesley collection)

and others on 18th April 1956, Bulleid enclosed a long list of items completed, including *inter alia*, reversing link blocks, a spindle for an oil pump and a sprocket retaining flange. If this was intended to halt the enquiries, it was in part successful as nothing more was heard from the Department for a further six months! The work was sufficiently advanced by March 1957 for the Chief Mechanical Engineer to arrange for Rex Roberts Studio in Dublin to make a slow motion film of the steam engine on test, "to ensure that there would be no irregularities on the valve motion...which is of new design". This was the first of at least three films made involving the Turf Burner; these films are now preserved in the National Railway Museum at York, but are currently unavailable for viewing.

Another review of internal transport within the Twenty-six Counties was carried out by a committee appointed in July 1956 by the Minister for Industry & Commerce. Chaired by J.P. Beddy, the committee's report was passed to the Minister in May 1957. Reference was made to the Government's approval in July 1953 of capital expenditure of £5.3million by the CIE board for the acquisition of 113 diesel locomotives, and the provision of the necessary oil storage facilities. The report also referred to proposals to construct fifty locomotives capable of operating either on oil or turf, once a satisfactory prototype had been developed. It was envisaged that these locomotives would normally operate on oil, but would be capable of operating on turf in an emergency; it was intended that they should be utilised for seasonal traffic such as sugar beet, or for the working of livestock specials. The Government considered the development

and provision of such locomotives should be regarded as a matter of prime importance, and to this end an additional sum of £1million was included in the CIE programme.

The new locomotive, almost complete, was towed from Inchicore to Kildare on 23rd May 1957 for riding tests with both Bulleid and Click aboard. The author was led to believe that two 101 class boilers were joined together at the firebox end for static steaming tests but neither Séan Heneghan nor his contemporaries can confirm this. We do know however that one of the engine units was fitted into a scrapped 101 class frame for steaming tests, steam being supplied from an old Aspinall 4-4-0; then with the engines installed in the bogies, the locomotive was steamed for the first time on 23rd July 1957. This was followed by a second steaming a week later. On this occasion, difficulties were encountered with the regulators, which could not be closed, and with the reverser. On the occasion of the third steaming on 4th August, the regulators worked satisfactorily, but the Westinghouse pump refused to operate. This unit had come from British Railways in Darlington in a repaired state, and had not therefore been tested before installation. On being removed and stripped down, it was found to be blocked almost solid with rust. Is it possible that some of Bulleid's old colleagues from the LNER were playing practical jokes on him, or were old scores being settled! The locomotive steamed and moved under its own power for the first time on Tuesday 6th August. Before we deal with this and the subsequent trials, it is time to take a look at the completed locomotive.

54

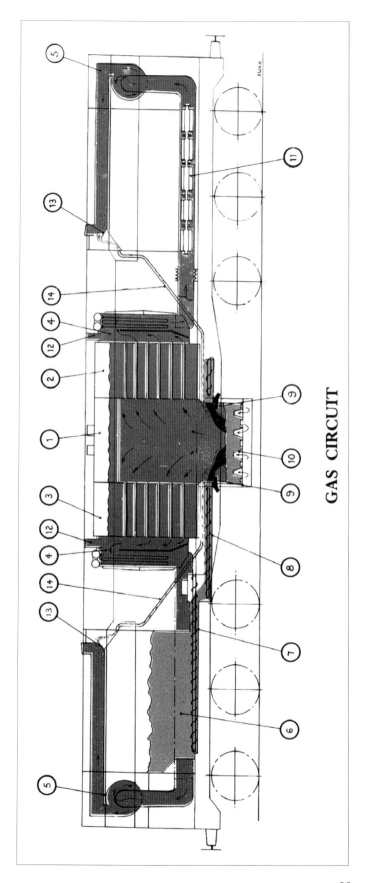

GAS CIRCUIT

1. Firebox section of boiler
2. Barrel section of boiler
3. Barrel section of boiler
4. Smokeboxes
5. Induction fan (turbine driven)
6. Turf supply
7. Hopper feed screw
8. Firebox feed screw
9. Jet plate
10. Firebars
11. Water feed heaters
12. Lighting-up chimney
13. Spark arrester
14. Spark return tube

The Gas Circuit

The mechanical stoker engine drives, through gearing, two turf feed screws (7) and (8) which convey turf from the hoppers (6) to the two entry points. Steam jets from the jet plates (9) distribute turf over the grate (10). The fire may be viewed through the firehole which is on one side of the firebox section of the boiler (1). Gases pass through tubes in the barrel sections of the boiler (2&3) and enter the smokeboxes (4). They are directed upwards by removable baffle plates and then down past the superheater elements. The gases leave the smokebox by right angled ducts at the corner of the smokeboxes (below the cab floor on the fireman's side) and passing through expansion bellows enter the heater duct in which are placed the aluminium feed water heaters (11). Leaving the heater ducts the gases pass upwards into the induction fan casings (5). Ducts from the fans lead to the outlets which are combined with spark arrestors (13). Particles caught by the spark arrestors are conveyed, via the flexible tubes (14) back to the firebox.
Note that although in the diagram only one pair of feed screws and one bank of heaters is shown for clarity, they were in fact fitted at both ends of the locomotive.

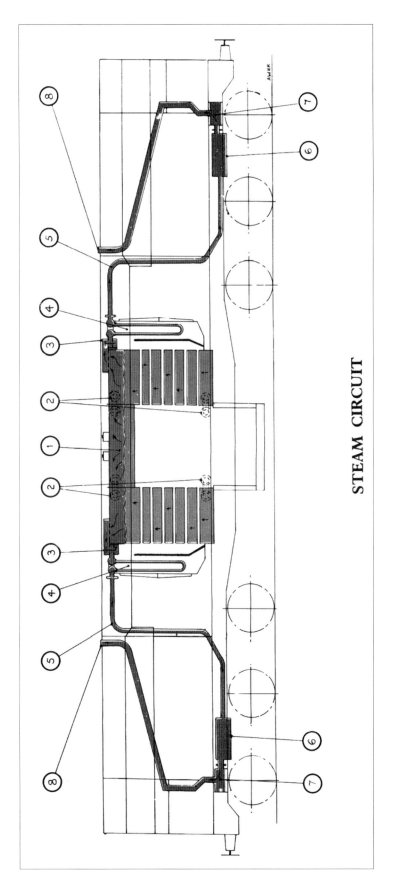

STEAM CIRCUIT

Steam generated in the firebox section of the boiler (1) flows into the steam space in the barrel section via the equalising pipes (2). Steam leaves the barrel and passes into a collector *en route* to the regulator valve (3). The steam then passes through the coils of the superheater (4) and into the flexible main steam pipe (5) which conveys it to the engine (6). The exhaust steam from the cylinder enters the bogie frame stretcher (7) which makes a faced joint with the main frame. Communicating slots in the stretchers allow the steam to pass away to atmosphere up the exhaust pipes (8).

1. Firebox section of boiler
2. Equalising pipes between boiler sections
3. Regulator valves
4. Superheaters
5. Main steampipes
6. Engine
7. Exhaust chambers in bogie segments
8. Exhaust steampipes

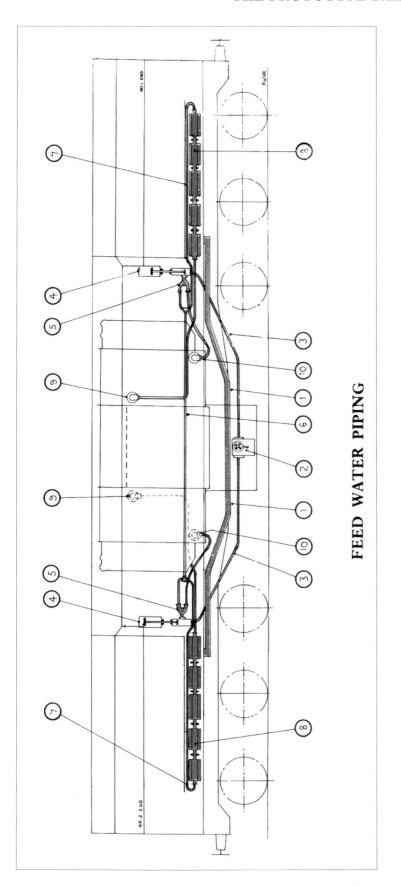

FEED WATER PIPING

Feed water from the water tanks at each end of the locomotive flows via the 4in diameter bore pipe (1) to the combined water feed valve and strainer (2). From here, suction pipes (3) carry the water to the Weir feed pumps (4). Leaving the pumps, under pressure, the water passes through two-way cocks, normally positioned to pass the water via the pipes (7) to the feed water heaters (8). In the event of emergency caused by leaking of the heaters, reversing the two-way cock causes water to flow into the boiler barrels via the emergency clacks (10). Normally water enters the boiler by the clackboxes (9). A balance pipe (6) connects the pumps so that either pump feeds both banks of heaters.

1. Balance pipe between water tanks
2. Water feed valve and strainer
3. Suction pipes to Weir pumps
4. Weir feed pumps
5. Heater isolating emergency cocks
6. Connection between pumps
7. Delivery pipe from pump to heaters
8. Water feed heaters
9. Clackboxes
10. Clackboxes (when heaters isolated)

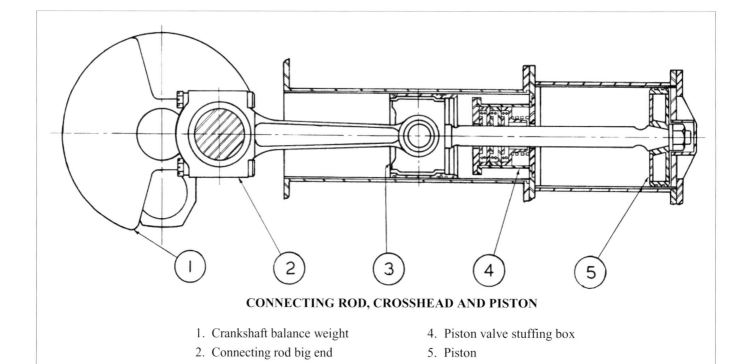

CONNECTING ROD, CROSSHEAD AND PISTON

1. Crankshaft balance weight
2. Connecting rod big end
3. Crosshead
4. Piston valve stuffing box
5. Piston

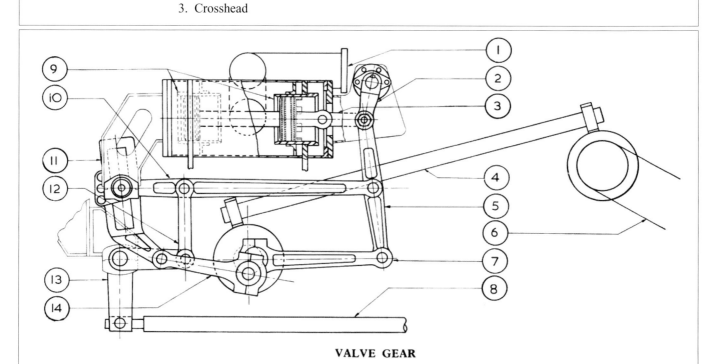

VALVE GEAR

1. Steam Inlet	6. Valve gear driving chain	11. Slotted link
2. Rocking arm	7. Combining lever motion shaft	12. Lifting link
3. Valve rod	8. Reversing rod	13. Weighbar shaft
4. Valve gear driving shaft	9. Piston valve and valve liners	14. Eccentric rod
5. Combining lever	10. Radius rod	

9

THE COMPLETED TURF BURNER

In a report prepared for Bulleid after the conclusion of the road trials, which is referred to in somewhat more detail later in our narrative, Click outlined the general criteria for the turf burner as follows:

1. It should be capable of operating almost system-wide on all classes of trains up to the maximum speed permitted on CIE lines.
2. It should have a high availability and be ready for work at short notice.
3. It should be able to run in either direction without turning, and its total weight should be available for adhesion and braking.
4. It should require little time for preparation, disposal and maintenance, and be straightforward to drive and fire.
5. In turf-burning mode, it should be mechanically fired to obviate the difficulties associated with hand-firing large volumes of turf.

The criteria were very similar again to that specified at the time Leader was built.

CC1 was soon numbered, although always generally known to all except Bulleid simply as "The Turf Burner". It is of interest to note that the three electric Co-Co locomotives built for the Southern Railway under Bulleid were numbered CC1, CC2 and 20003. The Turf Burner could be described simply as a double-ended locomotive carried on two six-wheeled bolsterless bogies, each driven by a removable two-cylinder simple steam engine with chain transmission. In this respect, it met criteria numbers 1 and 3 above. The locomotive's mainframe was 56ft 6in long, of completely welded construction throughout, the design making ingenious use of standard rolled-steel sections, cut, set and re-welded where necessary to achieve the desired profiles. Some of the cross-members required early modification to allow the stoker screw tubes to clear them.

The turf hopper and water tank had been completed quite a long time before the frame, and when the time came to weld these to the frame, it was discovered that they had far from level bottom plates. This necessitated what was referred to as 'brutal methods' to bring them sufficiently close-fitting to the frame. Whilst no leakages occurred during the subsequent trials, these plates must have been highly stressed and would no doubt in time have caused difficulties. A tank unit completely removable from the frame, would probably have been preferable. The hopper capacity was twelve tons of turf, and the water capacity 2,700 gallons. Unlike the Leader, the turf hoppers and water tanks were located at each end with the two driving cabs placed between them and the boiler. The cab sides and roof consisted of $^{1}/_{16}$in steel plate tacked to $^{1}/_{8}$in channel sections, the latter in turn being welded direct to the mainframe and to each hopper. The cab sides were unbraced over some 26ft except by the roof and this was to lead to severe vibrations at certain speeds.

The two six-wheeled bogies, each with a wheelbase of 12ft 7¾in, carried the mainframe and superstructure on three bearers. Some difficulty was experienced in positioning the bearers due to the fact that they could not be machined in position; in addition, the front bearer was at a different level to the two side bearers. The frame bearers were positioned with the frame inverted for ease of welding, but on being turned right-side up, it was discovered that it had twisted during fabrication. This necessitated tapered steel liners being fastened to the mainframe bearers to compensate for distortion in the frame and also to bring the bogies level despite the 'sag' in the frame. The bogie frames were made of 1in steel plate.

Wheels were of the Bulleid patent 'boxpok' type and were of 3ft 7in diameter. The three axles of each bogie were coupled externally by large, totally enclosed, chains, those connecting the inner and middle axles being on one side of the bogie, those connecting the middle and outer axles being on the opposite side. Bogie lubrication was provided by four mechanical lubricators driven by cranks on the free ends of the inner and outer end axles. A bronze liner with crossed oilways machined in it was screwed to the bogie top. Initially, engine oil was used but this proved unsuccessful, being squeezed out where local high pressure occurred and this led to some scoring. Cylinder oil was later substituted and proved to be satisfactory.

Each bogie contained a removable two-cylinder engine. The cylinders, measuring 12in by 14in, were fabricated rather than being cast (Ricardo at one stage enquired whether Bulleid was set on this, as he, Ricardo, much preferred castings, at least for the cylinder block) and the pistons were connected to the crankshafts by connecting rods only 2ft 1in in length. This short length was to be responsible for occasional difficulties encountered in setting back trains. The crossheads were unusual in locomotive practice, each consisting of a piston within a cylinder, rather than the conventional type guided by slide bars (see diagram at the top of page 58). This arrangement probably derived from marine practice, where double acting diesel engines were used. The crossheads had very large balance weights and the torque was transmitted by large chains to the layshafts geared to the inner axle of each bogie. Specially adapted Walschaerts valve gear was employed to drive the 7in diameter inside admission piston valves. These latter derived their motion from a single driving shaft driven by each crankshaft by means of a centrally positioned helical gear. This primary drive then drove another shaft below the cylinders.

At each end of this latter shaft, eccentrics operated the links at the front end of the cylinders and combining levers at the other end, which in turn drove the piston valves by means of rocking shafts. Cut-off and reversing were controlled by the links with the weighbar shaft fitted below the front end of the cylinders. Finally, valve travel was determined by the relative movement of the combining lever about the pivot formed by the valve rods and was varied by the adjustment of the reversing gear.

The crankshafts were of the built-up welded type. That in the No 1 engine (typically installed in the No 2 end bogie!) was machined using a portable crankpin skimming machine, and then finished by hand. This proved less than ideal and small cracks were found in the welds at the crankpin roots before installation into the engine. A similar machining was tried in engine No 2 but it was so misaligned as to prevent the assembled engine turning round. Eventually, a portion of the balance weights had to be cut off to allow the shaft to be ground on the main bearings and crankpins. The material salvaged from the balance weights had finally to be bolted back in position.

It was originally intended to have the valve gear in an oil bath, but it was later soft-grease lubricated. Engine sumps gave trouble with cracking at the corner welds. These were initially made of $1/16$ in plate but were subsequently doubled in thickness. Pressure fluctuations in the crankcase due to the crossheads caused constant breathing problems to occur, in turn resulting in fatigue failures.

Each bogie had its own steam circuit, all parts being duplicated. Steam reached the cylinders via 5in diameter flexible corrugated steel pipes, each pipe approximately 17ft in length, bolted by welded-on flanges to flanges on the superheater header and on the cylinder block. These pipes tended to twist slightly lengthwise to accommodate angular movements of the bogies beneath the frames. Initially, vertical vibration occurred to an alarming degree at No 2 end of the locomotive, this being all but damped out by fitting two hard rubber washers. Later, an omnibus body shock absorber was fitted to absorb transverse vibration at this end, the No 1 end not requiring any such treatment.

The boiler was centrally supported on the girder frame, and differed from that in Leader by being placed in the centre of the locomotive with the bunker and water tanks at each end, and with the two driving cabs placed between them and the boiler. All of these items were enclosed within the body, each cab having one access door on the left-hand side. Controls were duplicated in each cab. In addition the boiler was not off-centred with a passage way down one side as in Leader. The boiler itself comprised two square barrels located either side of a central firebox, the latter having a firedoor on one side only. As we shall see a little later, various types of firebar were tried, with air being provided by fans. As in Leader, the lower part of the firebox and the ashpan were lined with firebricks. Initially, no brick arch was fitted. The grate area was 22.8sq ft.

The two boiler barrels were connected over the top of the firebox with a water level of 9in above the crown.

There were 720 tubes of 4ft length and 1in diameter in each barrel, giving a heating surface of 1,484sq ft, to which was added 137sq ft from the firebox, a total of 1,621sq ft. The superheater contributed a further 320sq ft. Two 3in pop safety valves were situated above the firebox. The mechanical stoker drove, through gearing, two Archimedian feed screws which conveyed the turf from the hoppers to the two entry points. Steam jets distributed the turf over the grate. Each boiler barrel had its own smokebox, square to conform to the shape of the boiler, and containing a superheater, through which the gases were deflected by a baffle across the ends of the lower tubes. There were two smokebox doors, each opening into the adjacent driving compartment. Each smokebox also had its own chimney for lighting-up purposes, these being blanked off once steam was raised. Whilst ash blowers were fitted to the smokeboxes, they were never actually needed and were never used. Likewise it was seldom found necessary to open the smokebox doors as the boxes themselves were truly self-cleaning.

Gases passed through tubes in the two barrel sections, and entered the smokebox situated at the cab end of each barrel. Here the gases were directed upwards by removable baffle plates, and then down past the superheater elements. The gases then left the smokeboxes through right angled ducts at their corners (below the cab floor on the fireman's side), through extension bellows to enter a heater duct in which were placed aluminium feed water heaters. Leaving these ducts, the gases then passed upwards into the turbine driven reduction fans, and finally into the chimneys, one at each end of the cab. Spark arrestors were fitted, particles trapped by these being returned to the firebox through flexible tubes.

Steam generated in the firebox section of the boiler flowed into the steam space in the barrels. Leaving these, it passed via a collector to the regulator valve. The steam then passed through the superheater coils and into the flexible main steam pipes, which conveyed it to the engines. The latter consisted each of two cylinders 12in by 14in. The exhaust steam from the cylinders entered the bogie front stretchers, which made a faced joint with the main frame. Communicating slots in the stretchers allowed the steam to escape to atmosphere up the exhaust pipes.

The superheaters gave only a low degree of superheat, typically in the order of 100 to 120°F, and were of unusual design, consisting of a series of bends entirely within the smokebox gas area. This design was adopted because the original ideas omitted any form of superheating. We know that Bulleid was influenced to some extent by the Anderson Steam Cycle, developed by the late A.P.H. Anderson of Glasgow in about 1925. This had been experimentally tried on Southern Railway 2-6-0 No A816 in about 1930-4; it briefly comprised a means of converting exhaust steam into boiler feed water by condensing it, and pumping the water back into the boiler at a temperature of about 212°F. These experiments

THE COMPLETED TURF BURNER

CC1 in steam outside the Works in June 1958, probably the last date on which she was steamed.

failed due to insufficient draught at full load. It appears that Bulleid had considered the application of such a system to a locomotive similar in construction to the Merchant Navy class. It was not progressed however due to work on Leader, but it is on record that he had ideas of progressing these developments in Ireland.

Feed water from the water tanks at each end of the locomotive flowed via a 4in diameter pipe to a combined water feed valve and strainer. From here, suction pipes carried the water to the Weir feed pumps. Leaving the pumps under pressure, the water then passed through two-way cocks, normally positioned to pass the water via the pipes to the feed water pipes. However, in the event of an emergency due to leaking of the heaters, the cocks could be reversed to allow water to flow directly into the boiler barrels via emergency clacks. Normally water entered the boiler by means of clack-boxes. A balance pipe connected the pumps so that either pump could feed both banks of heaters.

The grate had special firebars, similar to those in No 356, known as tuyères, through which air for combustion was induced by means of draughting fans. The lower part of the firebox was lined with firebricks. Initially, there was no conventional brick arch, although two were fitted after about a month's trials, which greatly reduced the throwing of live sparks. It was feared that the fitting of the arches might tend to cause the lower rows of tubes to block, but this turned out not to be the case. The arch supports consisted of small pieces of steel bar welded directly to the firebox wall, thus exposing them to direct flame action. An improvement might have been effected by shaping the side brick and arranging to carry the weight of the arch by a bar; the support would not then be exposed to the flame action.

The grate was subjected to a number of modifications, each of which had the effect of improving steam production. The alterations included a progressive increase in the air space through the bars. A reduction in the number of tuyères was made, along with a reduction in their height. As first built the grate had similar proportions to that latterly fitted to No 356. As combustion rates increased during the trials, clinkering occurred; at its worst, a very heavy and dense clinker was produced. This led to the fitting in September 1957 of a rocking grate, operated in two sections, one for use on the road and the other for cleaning out. These alterations progressively increased the surface area of the bars from 32.9sq ft to 50.4sq ft, representing an increase in the ratio of flat to surface area from 1:1.44 to 1:2.22, the corresponding increase in the area of holes being from 3.66sq ft to 7.78sq ft.

Turf was contained in two large hoppers from which

BULLEID AND THE TURF BURNER

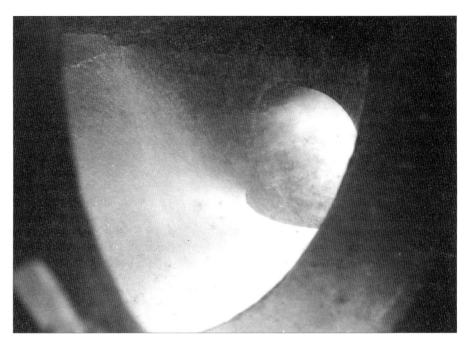

CC1 during trials. An unusual view showing exhaust sparks passing back to the firebox.

(G.F. Parrinder, G. Beesley collection)

it was fed by Archimedian screws into smaller hoppers from which it was delivered by a second pair of screws to the firebox. Distribution over the grate area was effected by steam jets. Initially, cast-iron jet plates were fitted, but these soon cracked due to thermal stresses. Turning the steam jets on caused condensate in the pipes to be suddenly introduced to the heated castings. These cast-iron plates were soon replaced by fabricated ones having the jets in a single group rather than in three, as in the original design. This simplified the controls, requiring only two cocks and two gauges in place of six of each. Trouble was also initially encountered with the fabricated plates due to blocked jets, this problem being cured by enlarging the holes. One essential was the even spreading of turf to prevent holes developing in the firebed. Once this occurred, they proved extremely difficult to fill. An added problem was that almost half of the grate was out of sight of the fireman, and out of reach with fire-irons – even the visible area could only be reached with great difficulty using a long rake. When a hole occurred, further feeding tended to aggravate the problem.

The locomotive was fitted with two Berkeley stokers, which functioned perfectly, always starting and running without noise, although they did transmit some vibration to the frames. Their capacity proved to be more than adequate to provide the boiler's needs and in fact one stoker would probably have sufficed. There was a tendency for burning back along the turf feed screw, this being avoidable if care was taken to ensure that they were run forward to deposit on the grate any smouldering turf above the jet plates, and then reversed, leaving gaps in the turf. Weir feed pumps were supplied to introduce water into the boiler.

Before finally feeding the firebox with the stokers, it was decided to blow turf over the grate with air supplied to the jets, whilst observing the results from inside the firebox. This immediately showed up something which would have been most difficult to observe and credit had the boiler been in steam. The earliest jet plate casting had a lip sloping upward at an angle of 30°, coming up at its highest point about 2½in from the bottom of the feed screw tube. Against this lip the stoker packed turf, which became almost as hard as wood and after a few turns the stoker stalled. The casting was immediately scrapped and testing was continued against a tin plate and copper tube mock-up which produced good results.

The brakes were of the Oërlikon type, brake power being provided by eight 8in diameter straight air cylinders positioned at the corners of the bogies. Each one actuated blocks on both sides of the wheel nearest to it and on one side of the centre wheel. Brake block carriers were standard with the Maybach diesel shunters and almost so with the A class Co-Co diesel electrics, of whose carriers they were a fabricated copy. We should mention here that Bulleid had always wanted to fit the Oërlikon brake. Click however tells the story that he had finally persuaded Bulleid late one afternoon not to go down this road, only to receive a telephone call from him first thing the next morning to the effect, "Oh, Click, fit the new (Oërlikon) brake, will you".

It is not known exactly when the number CC1 was applied to the Turf Burner, a photograph taken at Thurles on 4th October 1957 showed her devoid of them, while photographs taken a week later on 11th and 12th October clearly show them. She was only in the works for one day during that week for a boiler wash-out and the fitting of the small smoke deflectors. It may be of interest to note that the CC1 was variously referred to as the *Click Company of Ireland.* and *Click's Clever Invention*, neither very flattering to the locomotove's designer.

10

THE TRIALS

As already recorded, the Turf Burner took her first tentative steps on 6th August 1957, being confined to the Works yard where a speed of 25mph was achieved. On the following day, a second run was made, but disaster struck when she came into head-on collision with diesel-electric locomotive No 1100. Damage was sustained to the No 1 end buffer beam. It transpired that Click was in fact driving the Turf Burner on this occasion, being urged on by a shunter riding on the front footstep. Both saw the approach of No 1100 at the same time, the shunter diving off as Click applied the brakes. CC1 was virtually at a standstill when No 1100 struck at a speed estimated at about 12mph. Bulleid's first comment was that, "these things are sent to try us". A report was duly ordered into how this collision occurred. Click stated that on reading the report, Bulleid turned to him say-

ing, with a twinkle in his eye, " I understand both of you were stationary at the time of your little contretemps". Repairs were quickly carried out on the same day, enabling Bulleid and Monsieur Louis Armand, general manager of the Société Nationale Des Chemins De Fer Français (SNCF) and inventor of the TIA water treatment system, to ride on the locomotive up the yard at 30mph on the following day. A static boiler test two days later revealed that water levels were found to vary widely when the safety valve lifted. Between 10th and 12th August, additional packing was added to various glands and additional holes made in the jet plate.

The first run out on the main line was made on 13th August when a trip was made to Sallins with Bulleid on board, the locomotive reportedly performing well with the journey being completed without incident. The next day a

CC1 on load-starting trials leaving Inchicore on 27th September 1957 for Sallins. The five carriages are all of Bulleid design.
(Deegan-photo, copyright CIE)

BULLEID AND THE TURF BURNER

CC1 with five bogie carriages and a four-wheeled van en route to Cork on 4th October 1957 still in works grey livery. It was reported that the locomotive steamed better than ever before on this run. In addition, oil consumption was reduced although refilling was necessary at stops.

(G.F. Parrinder, G. Beesley collection)

light-engine run was made to Kildare and back, when a speed of 57 mph was attained. This time steaming was poor and there was slight heating of the axleboxes. The first load starting trials in the Works yard brought to light a problem with the burning of turf, when small lineside fires were caused by ejected particles. An intended run to Kildare on 16th August was halted at Newbridge after the roof of one of the carriages was set on fire. Despite this a speed of 63 mph was achieved on the return run. Some difficulties were being encountered with the reversing gear which required attention. About this time also, it was reported that Click had a seat welded onto the No 2 end bogie just behind the buffer beam, following which he rode below the locomotive at speeds in excess of 60 mph, including a round trip to Portarlington to observe the bogies, which rode perfectly satisfactorily at all speeds; this was the first occasion when comment was made regarding excessive oil leakage from the engines and cases. The Turf Burner was at this time in the charge of Driver Michael Keely of Inchicore, the fireman's name not being to hand. On a run to Clondalkin on 19th August it was reported that the cylinder

cocks had remained open due to bad machining.

Around this time, a number of runs were made to introduce the new toy to the chairman of CIE and officials of BnM. During the last three days of August, a number of runs were made to Sallins, Newbridge and Kildare to demonstrate the locomotive to Works officials and also to the Enginemen's Union officials. On this latter run the Westinghouse pump stuck repeatedly due to a broken valve ring. By the end of the month mileage stood at 613. During this period, modified steel firebars were fitted in place of cast-iron bars. This produced better steaming with higher temperatures, but it was also reported that severe priming occurred at the safety valves during running. More carriage roof fires occurred and two brick arches were fitted in an attempt to cure this problem, with some success. Another problem manifested itself about this time, a problem which had plagued all of Bulleid's designs, namely the serious oil leaks. There were also reports that difficulty was encountered in keeping the firebars covered with turf, arising from which some alterations were made to the distribution jets.

THE TRIALS

Following a run to Kildare on 4th September it was stated that the locomotive had steamed very well with five carriages and a van, "without carriage fires". Similar runs were made on the two following days. On each of the runs, the total evaporation rate was constant at between 13,000 and 14,000lb per hour. This appeared to be the limit of evaporation possible with the locomotive 'in the condition it then was'. As the loads increased on each successive day (160, 225 and 255 tons respectively), the timings to Kildare increased from 42 through 49 to 55 minutes. Turf consumption, including lighting up to 100psi, was calculated for the second and third runs at 84 and 99lb per train mile, this translating to 2.18 and 2.56 tons of turf respectively. Smokebox temperature was similar on each of the three runs, at 820°F, feed water temperature being 190°F.

The locomotive was then taken into the Works for a fortnight and was lifted for examination. The boxes in the bogies were reported to be in excellent condition, but rapid wear was occurring in the valve driving gears. The chain cases required some modification where the chains had made contact with them. In addition a rocking grate and spark arrestor were fitted, the latter being incorporated into the exhaust ducting. Finally, additional equalising pipes were fitted over the boiler top. Back on the road, 70 mph was attained for the first time, at Lucan, on a return trip from Sallins, riding being excellent at this speed. Interestingly the axleboxes were cooler than usual after a high-speed run. She then ran light to Cork on 25th September, returning the following day. Replenishment

CC1 photographed on an unknown date in October 1957 at Inchicore. The carriage next to the locomotive is a Bulleid designed composite in aluminium livery.

(Deegan-photo, copyright CIE)

From ground level, the difficulties involved in watering the engine due to the height of the water tank filler above rail level can be appreciated. As originally built, the access for this was via the end steps only, although later four steps were cut into the left hand end as seen here. Note all windows and door open in an attempt to reduce the heat in the cab.

(The late C.L. Fry)

CC1 passing No 1100 at an unknown location. This was the locomotive with which CC1 collided on 7th August whilst both loco-motives were apparently stationary! The leading four-wheeled van and the second, third and fourth carriages are Bulleid designs.

(The late C.L. Fry)

of oil from the sumps, "became (the) leading pre-occupation", although it was also reported that the jets at the No 2 end had become blocked at Thurles. On a further run to Sallins, oil loss was described as excessive, especially past the cross-heads. Back in the Works the sumps were strengthened and fitted with outside fillers, while the jet plate was again modi-fied. An interesting trip was made light engine on 2nd October to Mullingar and back, the one and only trial trip off the GS&W mainline. The constant curvature caused somewhat livelier riding but no extra heating of the axle boxes.

Another run was made to Cork two days later, with a load equal to 11 six-wheelers. Whilst oil consumption was reduced, the locomotive still needed refilling at stops. Leav-ing Cork on the return trip it was "touch and go in climbing the bank", although steaming was better than ever before. A high speed finish to the return trip was marred by the locomo-tive's failure to reverse the train across the road at Inchicore and she had to continue to Islandbridge. This was a problem also encountered with the Leader. Details of the up and down runs are to be found in Appendices J and K. Problems were also being encountered with smoke drifting down across the cab windows, a problem also common to the Bulleid Pacifics

on the Southern Railway not fully cured until the removal of the air-smoothed casing when rebuilt by BR. (Regarding the rebuilding of the Pacifics, Bulleid commented that he would have preferred the engines to have been scrapped rather than modified!) Smoke deflectors were now fitted to the No 1 end, and were sufficiently effective for the No 2 end to be done as well. It is clear from photographs that two types of deflector were in fact fitted, small and large, the former somewhat like those fitted to some of the L&NER Pacifics.

The locomotive's last trial referred to in the file was to Straffan on 16th October 1957. In the morning she ran light to Hazelhatch and back, having to stop at Clondalkin to re-move pieces of valve rings from a cylinder cock. Despite this, a run loaded equal to 7 was made to Straffan in the afternoon with Roland Bond and Bulleid's brother-in-law, H. G. Ivatt, on the footplate. With 2,147 miles accumulated, she was again lifted and it was found that four of the axle bearings had partially run the white metal.

11

THE CLICK REPORT

With the initial series of trials completed, Click submitted a lengthy and detailed report for Bulleid's consideration, although in the opening paragraph he concedes that it was in many respects premature, particularly since serious testing had not yet been undertaken. Up to 17th October 1957 a total of 2,147 miles had been run, all with one exception on the Cork mainline. The locomotive had been based at the Erecting Shop in Inchicore Works and had been serviced and maintained by Works fitters under the watchful eye of technical staff from the Drawing Office. In addition, it had been driven and fired by a selected crew from Inchicore Running Shed.

Under the heading of performance, results were generally very satisfactory and encouraging, having clearly demonstrated the locomotive's ability to burn poor quality turf sufficiently rapidly. Steaming however had never really been free but, "given close intelligent attention by an experienced fireman", an output of some 14,000lbs of steam per hour could be expected. Higher evaporation rates could be attained with better firing techniques coupled with improved grate arrangements. The locomotive rode excellently at all speeds up to 70mph. Much of the running had been at high speed and it was reported that signalmen were quite happy to let her away with only a short headway.

Turf consumption was not unduly high, with results being "very decidedly in favour of the new locomotive", a result which Click felt was particularly pleasing, as to be able to burn turf at all would previously have been regarded as an achievement. Furthermore, the turf provided had been of a poorer quality than that provided for No 356. Water consumption on the other hand was definitely on the high side for a modern locomotive. This was felt to be mainly attributable to the low superheat temperatures obtained, typically 100 to 120°F, although irregular valve events also tended to waste steam. Favourable comment had been placed on the locomotive's low noise level, to the point where it was suggested that the BR three-tone type whistle should be replaced by a standard CIE type.

Whilst the boiler had a number of good features to commend it, it was handicapped by being double ended; in addition, its sectional construction led to poor water circulation. The double ended arrangement made the use of very small tubes essential. Smokebox temperatures had been higher than desirable, yet not sufficient to make the superheater really efficient. The tubes were reported to have remained remarkably clean, only 15 out of the 1,440 becoming blocked throughout the trials. These were found to be blocked at the firebox end only and were easily cleaned by rodding. Likewise the smokeboxes remained clear of ash, the blowers never having been used.

Reference has already been made to the superheater. The superheater elements gave no trouble and appeared to be sufficiently well supported. Initially troubles were experienced with the regulators, which were sensitive but easy to operate. One of the problems encountered was the virtual impossibility of accurately synchronising the two regulators to give similar steam chest pressures at both ends under all working conditions. The driver required some skill in adjusting the regulators, a task performed by looking at the steam chest pressure gauge at the opposite end through a mirror in the corridor between the cabs. On some runs, a difference of 60 to 70 psi was recorded. Attention to the regulator valve was also difficult, necessitating as it did the prior removal of at least two pairs of superheater elements and the breaking of a steam joint in a very awkward position. As already recorded, no brick arches were fitted initially. Their subsequent addition considerably reduced the ejection of live sparks which had been responsible for several carriage roof fires. Whilst some ash tended to accumulate on the arch it tended generally to fall back to the grate rather than blocking the lower rows of tubes.

Many modifications were made to the grate during the trials, each one helping to improve the evaporation rate. The replacement of flat bars by the tuyères resulted in a more uniformly hot fire. Click conceded that there was still some room for improvements with the grate, particularly by further reducing the height of the tuyères and also enlarging the air spaces through them. Some difficulties were encountered with burning of the firebars and a slight change in design might overcome this problem. Click thought that for any new design the grate area should be doubled to achieve really good steaming.

Another item requiring frequent modification was that of turf distribution to evenly cover the grate and thus

Opposite page, top:
CC1 running light engine and approaching Straffan at speed on 11th October 1957. Note that since the photograph shown on page 64 was taken (a week earlier), she has been numbered. Two runs were made to Sallins on 11th October to test the lifting of smoke as the result of fitting small type smoke deflectors.

(G.F. Parrinder, G. Beesley collection)

Opposite page, bottom:
CC1 approaching Straffan light engine at speed on 12th October 1957. On the return trip from Kildare, she ran two hot boxes on the No 1 end bogie. Accumulated mileage now stood at 2,100.

(G.F. Parrinder, G. Beesley collection)

CC1 in its final form in full livery at Inchicore in June 1958. She was not steamed between mid-October 1957 and the end of May 1958. Click refers to problems encountered with poor balancing on short runs out as far as Hazlehatch in connection with a visit of the Institution of Locomotive Engineers in May. The view clearly shows the size of the engine, and illustrates the similarity in principal to the Fairlie ideal - two locomotives sharing a single firebox. Unlike Fairlie however, there was just the one boiler. Another deviation from the definition of a Fairlie was that the buffering and drawgear were affixed to the mainframe, and not to the bogies. Visibility for the crew was not ideal when running, although in practice it was little different to a number of other large steam classes. Despite the many criticisms, a feature of the engine was its superb braking. This was achieved with a combination of an air and vacuum system.
(Deegan-photo, copyright CIE)

avoid holes in the fire. To avoid the problem of uneven fire spread, any future design should have the firehole placed in such a position that the entire grate area could be observed by the fireman and enable him to use the fire irons effectively. One solution would be the provision of a single ended boiler, plans for which had already been drawn up (see page 78). Click commented that despite all the difficulties and the uncomfortable location, two regular firemen had obtained good results.

The ashpan was brick lined and this had stood up well during the tests. Once hot, it and the brick arch helped to maintain the temperature of the firebed. It was noted that the outside of the ashpan never became unduly hot, a tribute to the heat insulating properties of the bricks used. In fact, the only external heat problem was with the lugs for the smokebox doors which became extremely hot. The TIA water treatment caused major problems as regards boiler wash out as the flat base of each barrel acted as a collector for mud. This latter, although soft, proved difficult to remove due to the number of stays which effectively broke up any jet of water directed at the mud through the washout plugs. Inspection and thorough cleaning of the firebox water legs was not possible as the lowest plugs were almost a foot above the base plate.

There was no tendency for the boiler to prime, except through the safety valves, despite the fact that the water levels were on occasions higher than was necessary or desirable. It was reported that on one occasion the water level in the firebox section rose, while the safety valves were lifting, high enough for water to enter the auxiliaries' stop-cocks. This had the effect of stopping the pumps, resulting in a greater quantity of steam reaching the turbines, a condition which prevented water being put into the boiler just when it was most needed. The fitting of equalising pipes over the top of the boiler cured the problem of safety valve priming. Boiler mountings in general drew little comment. The Weir pumps, which appear to have operated satisfactorily in No 356, were temperamental in working, often stopping for no apparent reason. Part of the problem was probably due to the temperature of the water coming from the tanks – they commenced hammering when the water temperature reached about 140°F. The last few hundred gallons of water in the tank was prone to become very hot due to the heating effect of the gas ducts, resulting in pump failure.

Unlike those fitted to No 356, the aluminium alloy feed heaters gave no trouble due to leakages. Click considered the feed heaters to be of limited use and suggested the alternative of heating the feed water from the exhaust steam, which with the use of fan draughting did nothing useful. The two turbo-fan sets gave no trouble in operation, with gases up to 500°F passing through them for long periods. The turbines were much larger than was necessary and it was believed that one would have sufficed. As it was, they never received steam at more than 125psi, and two nozzles out of three in each casing had been blanked off. The turbines did use a lot of steam at

Bulleid and Click, no doubt in deep conversation....

low speeds and pressures and it was recommended that pressure be brought up to about 100psi and the stokers started before the turbines were started.

Initially, a considerable volume of live sparks was ejected from the exhaust. To overcome this, a spark arrestor was incorporated into the outlet which trapped large particles and returned them through a flexible tube to the firebox. Also, it was decided to carry the exhaust duct back horizontally below the turf space roof and to position the outlet just ahead of the cab. The exhaust pipes from the engines, stokers, turbines, Weir pumps and the Westinghouse pump were all repositioned, the auxiliaries exhausting into the engine exhaust.

On the question of sighting by the driver and fireman, no problems were encountered on straight track with both men having good views ahead and comfortably seated behind windows which were generous in size compared with those in the 400 and 800 classes. With No 2 end leading however, both driver and fireman were on the same side of the locomotive. Difficulties were encountered in entering goods yards and locomotive depots for the purpose of coupling up to other stock, and some attention would need to be directed to this for the future. Drifting steam was an early problem. The decision to bring the exhaust out just ahead of the cab resulted in the view from the driver's window being seriously obscured by steam and smoke blowing down under certain damp weather conditions, and smoke deflectors had to be fitted. Photographs indicate that at least two types of deflector were in fact fitted. One down side of the fitting of smoke deflectors was that the filling of the water tanks became more difficult, making hand holds fitted in the tank sides desirable to allow access by the fireman.

Click considered that the bogie frames, which were of

View in cab of CC1 taken on the occasion of the visit of the Institution of Locomotive Engineers to Inchicore on 15th May 1957. Left to right are Robert Arbuthnot (North British Locomotive Co Glasgow, who were the builders of No 356), C.S. Cocks (BR) and Driver Michael Keely. CC1 had two regulators, one per cab, but only one firehole. This meant that the crew would only work together when the engine was being worked one way. Complexities with the mechanical linkage necessary to secure the regulator in the unused cab out of action was one of the reasons for the later proposal for a single cab version of the Turf Burner.

(Lensmen, CIE)

1in steel plate, were, "rather heavy for the somewhat flimsy structure they are". The bogies were not very rigidly braced and the only contribution the engines made was to the lateral bracing where they were fixed to the bogie plates at the top of the crankcase. The August collision with No 1100 demonstrated the need for some strengthening of the original buffer beams, there having been no stiffening between the main and secondary frame members. Weight could have been saved by using thinner section for the hoppers, water tanks, cab sides and roof.

The engines themselves did all that was required of

them. Frequent high speed runs were made, often at over 500rpm. Their maximum effort was when lifting the test train up the bank out of Cork. However they suffered in Click's view by having only two cylinders and the fact that an undesirably high percentage of reciprocating balance had been applied. The two cranks, at 90° to one another, caused severe pumping action in the crank cases and ahead of the crossheads. The lubrication of the main bearing big ends and the intermediate shaft bearings was successful in running, although oil loss proved to be an insuperable problem with the existing design. Pressure oil feeds over the crosshead guides

CC1 at an Inchicore Open Day in June 1958. On the left is one of the AEC diesel railcars. Two, including this one, were experimentally painted with the yellow stripes to improve visibility for permanent way men.

(Photographer unknown, G. Beesley collection)

and to the small ends were found to be essential to prevent heating and binding during running-in. The connecting rods were too short and caused some difficulties in setting back trains, a problem also encountered with Leader. The use of Walschaerts valve gear was good, but valve events suffered due to the shortness of the rods.

Initial boiler testing before the road trials began indicated that the water gauge levels fluctuated very widely. These were in fact false readings, and were due to the inadequate equalising pipe area originally provided in the steam space between the boiler sections. Both of the engines were tested in steam, using an old 4-4-0 locomotive as a stationary boiler. No 1 engine was initially fitted into a scrapped 101 class frame, inverted and cut to suit. It was found necessary to make many adjustments before smooth running was obtained. Speeds of up to 250rpm were obtained before vibration became too pronounced. Both engines were subsequently run under steam in their own bogies before being placed under the locomotive.

Before No 356 was scrapped (in 1957), the opportunity was taken to carry out tests with one of the turbo-fan sets for draught purposes. These tests were however curtailed due to breakdowns with the stoker. Both Weir pumps from No 356 were subsequently fitted in the prototype after stripping and repair. Reference has already been made to the initial problems with the Westinghouse pump.

The lightweight brake cylinders contrasted with the overly heavy rigging, from which a great deal of weight could be taken. Air was supplied from a compressor in the No 1 end cab. The fact that the locomotive was fitted only with the air brake was drawn to the attention of drivers by means of a prominent cast plate. With a vacuum braked train, it would be all too easy for a driver to move off when the train pipe was exhausted without an air supply. Hand brake wheels were positioned on the bogie frame on the corner nearest to the cab entrance doors. Click commented that "they could only be applied, whilst running, by a feat of gymnastics not to be dwelt upon". Despite the fact that the hand brake wheels were painted white and had large red arrows in relief pointing out that the brakes were applied by turning them clockwise, most newcomers were observed spinning the wheels hard off to apply the brakes. It was recommended that in any new design, the hand brake wheel be positioned in the cab within easy reach in the event of an emergency.

The system of disconnecting the regulator handle that was not in use by removing a latch pin and clipping the handle back out of the way presented no problems. A similar arrangement could be used from side to side of the proposed single cab design. The Hadfield steam reverser was controlled by levers at each end, simultaneously connected to the valve operating lever on the reverser itself. The cab levers had an indicator pointer travelling over a sector plate to indicate cut-off. The lever was pulled in the desired direction just sufficient to open the steam and oil valves. A definite check had to be given to the lever in order to stop the reverser, and to prevent it creeping into full gear. Should the reversing lever be pulled sharply, the reverser valves opened too widely and the locomotive went immediately into full reverse. On the new design, it was suggested that the power reverser should be controlled by a combined latch and screw, the former to give full forward and reverse, the latter for making fine adjustments to the cut-off. Thus easy reversing would be available for shunting and accurate positioning with no danger of the reverser running away. To provide a similar arrangement on both sides of the cab would however call for some ingenuity.

The cylinder cocks worked well, there being only one reported refusal to close – this was due to a large piece of piston valve ring being found lodged in it. Vertical pull chains were provided to operate the whistle. The ideal would be a pushbar within range of both the driver and fireman. No sanding gear was fitted, nor was it necessary, although some slipping had occurred when oil had spilt on the rails from the sump.

Short shunting movements sometimes proved to be difficult. At least 150psi steam chest pressure was found to be necessary to start the locomotive. It then tended to move further than desired due to the large volume of steam in the steampipes and chests, even with the cocks opened and the regulator closed as soon as movement commenced. It was suggested that the main steampipes could with advantage be reduced to 4in diameter. It was also suggested that a scrap 800 class tender could be modified by being cut down to the level of the locomotive's water tank top and closely coupled rigidly to it. It is perhaps of interest to note that No 802 was scrapped in 1957. Was her tender earmarked for use behind CC1?

The axleboxes were of solid bronze with white-metal inserts, running on plain journal bearings. Oil was supplied by a six-feed Wakefield mechanical lubricator feeding into the underkeep. From the beginning, the boxes ran warm every time the locomotive ran at high speed. This was not entirely surprising as at 70mph, the 547rpm corresponded to a speed of 132mph in a locomotive having 6ft 9in driving wheels. After the light return run to Kildare on 12th October 1957, the left driving axlebox in No 2 bogie was very badly heated – almost on fire. It was believed that the wheel boss lubrication had been defective as felt pads of unsuitable quality had been used. A change of axle oil to pure rape seed oil was made at this time.

It was recommended that in any future design, provision should be made for overhead oil connections in the castings. Water was on occasions found in the axlebox keeps, most likely as the result of allowing the water tanks to overflow. Hot boxes were difficult to deal with, even in the Works, as this necessitated emptying the turf hoppers, disconnecting the main steam pipes, lifting the superstructure off the bogies and then un-wheeling the offending bogie. Thus, heating anywhere on the system required the locomotive to be brought back to Inchicore for attention. It has to be said however that a similar situation applied to locomotives of the 372, 400, 500 and 800 classes. Roller bearing axleboxes were considered necessary in the new design.

Drive from the engines and coupling of the wheels was, as we have seen, by chains. The primary chain coupled the right hand end of the crankshaft to the intermediate shaft. The oilcase surrounding this chain was in three sections. It suffered badly from leaks where it was fitted into grooves in the bearing bushes. The problem of arranging an oil-tight case between the intermediate shaft and the rear axle was overcome by allowing the case itself to run on the axle. The method of supporting the case by an extension of the intermediate shaft proved troublesome due to side to side movement of the case, which caused the bolts holding the extension in place to fail. In future, the drive should be made on to the centre axle without the complication of the intermediate shaft. The coupling chains sagged during the trials almost to the point of allowing them to touch the casing, that is, a sag of about ¾in after a mileage of just over 2,000. This was despite great care being taken in spacing the wheelbase accurately in the bogies. Water got into the cases during tank filling and emulsified the oil. The chains also suffered severe snatching on occasions when reversing, this obviously also contributing to the sag. Oil had to be constantly added to the sumps to maintain a safe level. For example on the run to Cork, this had to be done at Portarlington, Thurles, Kilmallock and Mallow. An oil drum was carried in the cab for this purpose. Even on a good day the oil loss worked out as at least a gallon every 10 miles.

Provision was made for electric lighting by means of a generator belt driven off the inner axle of No 1 bogie, a bracket having been welded to the bogie rear plank. Oil leakage would have necessitated the provision of a cover plate to protect the belt and pulley from oil. A battery box was also fitted and was conveniently used as a toolbox. It had been

THE CLICK REPORT

CC1 at the turf-loading conveyor at Inchicore on 1ˢᵗ September 1957. She had been in the Works on the previous two days having two brick arches fitted. Her boiler was found to be very dirty when washed out.

(N.C. Simmons)

intended to fit two white lights above each buffer beam as well as cab lighting for both the driver and fireman.

Fuelling was carried out by hand at the Erecting Shop, turf being supplied from Clonsast by lorry in 1cwt bags. These bags were manhandled from the lorries into condemned covered goods wagons for storage, being finally tipped, again by hand, into the locomotive's hopper. So much handling was a very costly procedure and special installations would have been required at locomotive sheds.

Converting to oil would have been relatively simple. The boiler was considered to be ideally suited to firing by a Laidlaw-Drew type burner placed centrally in the firepan. In fact one had been designed specifically for the locomotive. None of the firebox heating surface would be lost by being bricked over since a deep enough firepan could be provided to contain the flame cone. As we have seen already, CIE had amassed enough information on oil burning and it seemed hardly worth while converting the prototype to oil. Greater evaporation rates would be obtainable with oil and the locomotive's range extended. Two alternative suggestions were

put forward. Two small burners might be used, or the rear part of the firepan could be blocked off and a single burner used in a deep pan at the front of the firebox.

In conclusion, Click was in no doubt as to the feasibility of a fleet of turf burning steam locomotives operating economically. However, only a drastic re-design and redisposition of the major components in the prototype could result in the quantity production of machines simple enough to operate and maintain. That said, the prototype was capable of doing useful work. When all the data and experience that could usefully be extracted had been obtained, the locomotive should be withdrawn as its purpose would have been served. The good work performed by the prototype in large measure resulted from the exceptional attention given to the locomotive by all those responsible, especially the chargehand fitter. In the absence of such attention the design as it stood would have soon been in difficulties.

Two main weaknesses were inherent in the prototype. The boiler had insufficient grate area and was exceedingly difficult to fire. Turf could not be burned quickly enough to produce sufficient steam, nor could the firebed temperature be maintained high enough to sustain rapid combustion owing to the constant addition of fresh turf. The second drawback was the symmetrical arrangement of the locomotive about its centre line, resulting in two hoppers, tanks, cabs, boilers, stokers, turbines and fans. This was unnecessarily extravagant in space and weight, both of which were at a premium.

A design for a single ended locomotive of similar capacity for less all-up weight would be possible. At the same time, water capacity would be increased, turf capacity being slightly less however. The crew would have been together in a roomy cab with good vision in both directions. A single ended square section boiler barrel with a large water legged firebox, possibly incorporating arch tubes, and a brick lined firepan was to be provided. This boiler would have a high degree of superheat from a conventional superheater. A Henschel Feed Heater would be employed. To assist in weight distribution only, water would be divided between tanks at each end of the locomotive. The engines, preferably each of three cylinders, should be arranged so as to have the main drive incorporated in the crankcase and on to the centre axle. Valves and pistons would be positioned so as to allow of inspection from pit level. Finally, roller bearing axleboxes should be fitted.

Such a locomotive, with the component parts reduced to a minimum, could then be cheaply produced with interchangeable bogies and engines. The TIA equipped boiler would require little maintenance, and engines would be substituted at 50,000 miles to allow for inspection and attention to valves and pistons. Down time would be kept to a minimum. This would result in a general purpose locomotive capable of burning indigenous fuels – turf or anthracite – for lines with low traffic density, light axle loading, heavy gradients combined with sharp curves requiring good adhesion, and where electrification and dieselisation would not justify their much higher capital expenditure. Click even envisaged attractive possibilities abroad.

After the Trials

The report ended on an up-beat note, but this was to be effectively the end of the turf-burning experiment. It is reported that CC1 did subsequently make a few trips on the transfer goods between North Wall and Kingsbridge in the early months of 1958, although proof of this is lacking. She was exhibited at Inchicore in May and June 1958 in connection with the summer meetings of the Institution of Locomotive Engineers and the Institute of Transport. On the occasion of the May visit, Bulleid himself reportedly drove the Turf Burner up and down to Clondalkin, giving footplate rides to various visiting dignitaries. This was the only occasion on which he had driven the engine himself, although he had apparently travelled on it on several previous occasions.

Bulleid retired on 30th May 1958 at the age of 75 and

this was as good an opportunity as any for abandoning the testing. The Department for Transport & Power wrote in June 1961 regarding developments with the turf-burning experiment. A note at the bottom of a memorandum from Lucas Collins, the mechanical engineer, reads simply, "Project abandoned as completely uneconomic, Department advised". Click had apparently been involved up to May 1958, having been out on a short trip to Hazlehatch, when he found the valve settings prevented running with the reverser pulled up below 40%. He also felt the balancing of the crankshafts was not right as thumping occurred at about 40mph. The reason undoubtedly was that the locomotive had been rushed out of the shops for the visit of the Locomotive Engineers later in the month.

In a letter to Bulleid early in June 1958, Click, who had by now returned to British Railways (BR), informed him that BR had no objection to him (Click) going to Inchicore during the annual shut-down of the Rugby Test Plant in July. Why he should write so to Bulleid after the latter's departure from Inchicore is unknown. He suggested further tests to accurately establish the amount of steam used by the turbo-fans, one of which should be supplied with steam from a train heating van boiler. In this letter, Click commented that, "If one impression remains with me more than another it is of the loyal way in which those few did everything to push the job on. The driver and chargehand were the best I ever came across. Nothing was too much trouble the other week for them and they worked outside in three of the worst days I remember at Inchicore". Praise indeed from Click!

Forty years on, what can one say of the Turf Burner? By 1958, CIE had more than 100 main and branch line diesel-electric locomotives in service. 15 more, this time from General Motors, would be introduced three years later. Bulleid's retirement certainly brought an end to any further trials. CC1 undoubtedly had too many departures from conventional steam locomotive construction practices and it seems unlikely that it would ever have been made a success without many modifications. Time had however run out for steam traction. Apart from this, as Click commented, the locomotive had been looked after and was worked by a dedicated team at Inchicore. This treatment could not be given to a fleet of such locomotives. CC1 versus Metrovick might look good, but compared to the performance and reliability of the 'GMs', it was not a viable proposition. Following the delivery of a further 37 GM locomotives in 1962, the locomotive was officially withdrawn in 1963 and broken up shortly afterwards. The boiler was retained for possible stationary use.

The principal reason for not pursuing the turf-burning project was, without doubt, Bulleid's departure from Inchicore. As we have seen, the dieselisation programme was well under way and this also would have affected thinking and decision making. Click really signed CC1's death warrant when he commented on the specialised treatment meted out to Bulleid's plaything. There could be no justification for con-

THE CLICK REPORT

The End! CC1 at Inchicore on 10th May 1962 quietly rusting and awaiting breaking up. She had not been steamed for some four years at this point.

(S.C. Walsh)

tinuing an experiment that required dedicated crews and maintenance staff, with the attendant expense. This combination of factors put an end to what had been little more than another opportunity for Bulleid to exercise his inventive brain and spend somebody's money along the way. Apart from this altogether, the writing was on the wall worldwide for steam traction, except for those few countries that had large reserves of indigenous fuels, such as China and South Africa. Even in these countries, conventional steam locomotives were built with modifications to reduce the cost of operation.

It has been said of Bulleid that he was, "an expensive and irresponsible Chief Mechanical Engineer who pursued novelty for its own sake and had no interest in providing his company with genuine traffic engines". Perhaps this was true of his locomotives, but the same cannot be said of his rolling stock. During his time with CIE, a large number of carriages and wagons were constructed, which gave long and excellent service.

We shall leave the last word to Roland Bond, who had moved from the LMS at Derby to join Robert Riddles' team at Railway Executive Headquarters in January 1948. Bond had seen Leader at Eastleigh in June 1949 and was later to be invited to Inchicore with Bulleid's brother-in-law, H.G. Ivatt, to see the Turf Burner. He commented in his autobiography that Bulleid, "must often have been up in the clouds exercising his inventive mind on new and original ideas". He then went on to say that, "We could not but admire Bulleid's persistence and marvelled as much at his manifest ability to extract money from Boards of Directors as at his unquenchable addiction to technical innovation". This it seems is a fitting comment on which to close the story of "The Turf Burner". However, in the light of the ESB's success with conventional steam plant, one wonders what the outcome might have been if turf firing of a conventional steam locomotive design had been pursued with the enthusiasm applied to the novel design features of the Turf Burner.

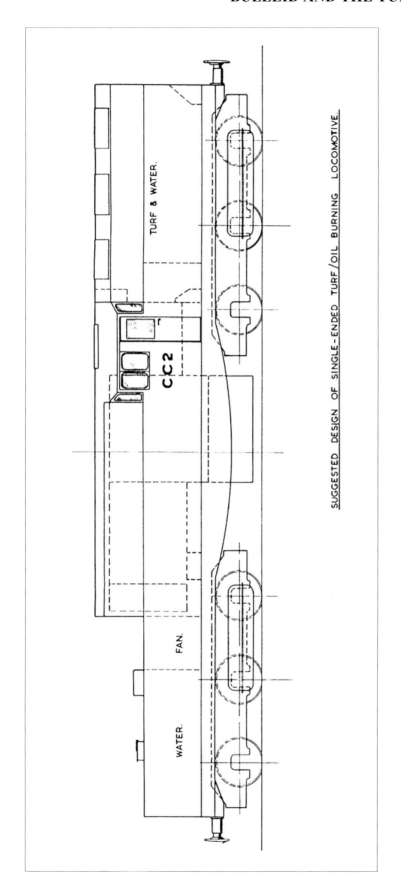

SUGGESTED DESIGN OF SINGLE-ENDED TURF/OIL BURNING LOCOMOTIVE.

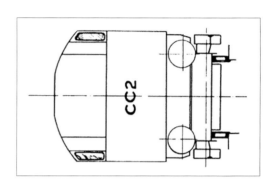

Plan of proposed single ended Turf Burner. The plan is both undated and unsigned although may well be the work of Click. A sketched drawing of a similar proposal is located within the NRM archives.

Report on CIE Locomotives Prepared in 1948 in Connection with Boiler Renewals

<u>Class 545.</u> Number in class 5. A class boiler. (Henceforward shown as, for example, 5/A.) Built as passenger engine. Their passenger loading is too small for main line work and their axleload precludes them from working branch lines such as D&SE to Wexford where the load would suit. They are used as goods engines (chiefly Cattle and Special Goods) but no 4-4-0 engine is efficient on such work. They work local passenger trains in Cork area. A poor design, slow and unreliable, suitable for slow stopping trains of about 150 tons.

<u>Class 623.</u> 23/C. A powerful engine, primarily used on goods work for which they are suitable. They can work passenger trains such as the 372 class work on the Midland section. On this work their life is short. All engines of class are on Midland section. Upkeep rather heavy.

<u>Classes 540 & 536.</u> 5 & 4/C. These are similar and interchangeable on work. They are similar to the 545 class except 536 class has a smaller boiler, 540 class slightly larger. Sluggish, bad running engines. Can run on D&SE section but cannot keep time.

<u>Classes 372 & 393.</u> 20 & 6/D. Primarily goods engines but suitable for passenger trains. The only difference in the classes is the 393 have larger wheels. They work Galway passenger trains but are too overloaded to run fast; also Sligo passenger and Rosslare expresses, up and down Cork night mails. The boilers were built for British gauge and are too small for Irish requirements. Their axle load is much in their favour because they can go over sections that other large engines cannot. A good general purpose engine not requiring excessive repair.

<u>Class 551.</u> 12/E. A small tank engine suitable only for shunting. Very small boiler, coal and water capacity, however, limits their use in that field. Three engines on self-contained Waterford/Tramore Section.

<u>Class 619.</u> 3/H. A very powerful engine, but the wheel diameter is 4ft 9in from which the higher power is derived; the revolutions per mile are, therefore, excessive and the engine needs continuous heavy repair after 20,000 miles.

<u>Class 222.</u> 4/J. (Same boiler in 234, 276 & 296 classes.) These are similar to the Standard Goods classes but smaller. Their loads are, of course, less and they are only suitable for small branches or specials.

<u>Class 234.</u> Only one of its class. Similar to Standard, but slightly smaller. Does shunting work.

<u>Class 276.</u> 4. A very light passenger engine suitable only for Branch lines or Pilots. Obsolete type.

<u>Class 296.</u> 2. Similar remarks to those re 234 and 276 classes; obsolete.

<u>Class 400.</u> 7/K & 400. Can work main line trains up to load of 20, night mail or goods. Given a high maintenance standard and load of 12-14 could run fast service. They are not all of a standard design. There are 2 with Caprotti gear, 1 with Walschaerts & 4 others rather similar. Can only work 100 tons on fast Cork service (about 2h 50m) Would suit as heavy goods engines for many years.

<u>Class 500.</u> 3/K & 400. Can work any train worked by 400 class. Have in the past worked Cork Mail but small diameter wheels renders them quite unsuitable for such work. Better on goods work than passenger, except on night mails.

<u>Class 800.</u> 3/M. Good fast engines, needing little repair. Only three however in class which reduces their value. Limited Cork to Kingsbridge. If one was in shops and two working one fast train each way daily, it could not be replaced if unable to work return trip.

<u>Classes 301-310.</u> 4 & 6/N. (Also in 257, 351, 211, 442, 454, 455 & 213 classes.) Perform almost similar work. Suit local passenger trains in the Districts. Not much use for goods trains. Given suitable load can run quite fast.

<u>Class 257.</u> 8. These are a very good engine for goods working, economic and with a long life. Axle load gives them a wide range. I would like to see half the 101 class scrapped and many other stray goods classes, and replaced by this design.

<u>Class 351.</u> 7. Comparable in size with above, but a bad design of valve gear makes them heavy on coal and sluggish. They have a

short economic life in consequence.

Class 211. 2. On paper very powerful but power obtained by too small wheel (or low gear) with the result they have short economic life. Suitable only for goods on undulating lines such as D&SE, Mallow/Waterford and Mallow/Tralee sections. Only two in class.

Class 442. 4. A D&SE edition of Standard Goods. Quite good.

Class 454. 1. A nondescript engine and only one of class. Consequently difficult to place, otherwise it is a fair medium powered passenger engine.

Class 455. 3. D&SE heavy passenger service engines. Well maintained - not at all bad. Essential to local services. Not powerful enough to enable speeding up of the local services with loads of six bogies (equivalent to twelve 30 footers).

Class 213. 2. A tank edition of 211 class. Primarily shunter, but used as expedient on Cork/Bandon section, being a tank engine and low axle load.

Classes 305, 306 & 307. 3/O. For practical purposes these are same class. They are suitable for medium passenger trains, such as Waterford/Limerick, Mallow/Tralee etc.

Classes 333 & 343. 8 & 5/O. Similar - valuable because they are fairly powerful and can travel most lines with their 16 ton axle load. Very useful for passenger specials. Reasonable fast, 342 class completed about 1936. Generally these will perform the same work as 321 class. Not suitable for sustained high speed except with light loads and thus employed have a short life. Too many types within the classes.

Classes 355 & 368. 6 & 2/Q. Very useful heavy goods engines, powerful and with a low axle load enabling them to be worked over many lines. A type which should have been developed.

Class 463. 6/R. These were engines built for Bandon Railway. They are primarily small but powerful passenger engines, suitable for Cork/Bandon services. They also work goods on that section. One is on the D&SE section, but it is a little too small for that section. Quite good design.

Classes 269 & 295. 4 & 1/S. Obsolete small passenger engines suitable only for small branches and Cork/Bandon section, light shunting. Used as an expedient rather than by choice.

Classes 423-428. 3 & 5/Tipperary. All these engines (D&SE and occasionally one or two on Cork/Bandon or shunting at Mallow) are obsolete in every way. They are slow and high in coal consumption. The number in service limits the performance of the whole D&SE local service. With some alterations would suit as shunting pilots.

Class 2. 8/U. Quite a good design of very light passenger engine, but for which there is an ever decreasing demand. They are used between Limerick and Sligo but are too low in power even for that service. Useful for assisting trains.

Classes 33-37. 6 & 6/U. Small passenger tank engines of obsolete design. Used on Cork/Bandon section.

Class 321. 9/W. A good medium passenger engine, capable of similar work to 333 class, but has larger wheel and boiler, consequently faster, but high axle load is a disadvantage. Maximum speed approximately 68mph. Useful for newspaper trains.

Class 52. 18/X. Similar to 2 class. Suits Kildare/Kilkenny and Sligo/Limerick. Too small. They are at present limiting the speed of Branch trains which must be worked by them. No use for goods working.

Class 530. 5/X. Completely obsolete. Small passenger engine of bad design. Same remarks as 52 class.

Classes 573-594. 15 & 19/X. The Midland edition of the 101 class Standard Goods. Design poor and very few of them alike. Wear too rapidly. Essential to keep working.

Class 567. 1/X. Only one of type. Was built from 573 class as an experimental development which was justified, but not continued. A good engine.

Class 614. 5/X. Small shunting tank engine, only suitable for small yards and short banking trips. Obsolete.

Class 27. 4/X. Small obsolete tank passenger engine, used mainly on Cork/Bandon and Cork/Cobh lines.

Class 650. 19/Y. Quite a good small passenger engine which will work most Midland branches and some D&SE section local trains. Slightly better than 2, 52 & 530 classes and for their size do good work but they are slow and suited for very few modern trains.

Class 101. 96/Z, 60 & 101. The general purpose small Goods engine can work over most lines. There are many variations within the class. Will also work Branch Passenger trains and, where assisted, Sunday Specials off low axle load branches.

Class 60. 15/Z & 60. Small passenger engine, fast and reliable. Suitable for Branch Passenger trains and trains such as former Newspaper trains, on which with loads of about 75 tons can sustain 60mph for long periods. An ideal engine with which to dou-blehead another underpowered engine, such as 333 class on a limited axle load Branch. Economical to work and maintain.

Classes 201-204. 10 & 1/101 & 60. Powerful tank shunting engines, eminently suitable for heavy goods yard and banking of trains.

Class 670. 5/Z. This is a tank edition of 710 class tender engine used entirely on D&SE section. They are slow and need too much repair. Could not, however, work D&SE section without them.

Class 434. 6/101 & 434. Obsolete D&SE section passenger engine.

Class 700. 5/700. Built in 1929 as an addition to 101 class, but from running point of view it did not compare with older design.

Class 710. 10/Z. Intended as a modern addition to 101 class. Reasonably good.

Class 458. 3/458. D&SE heavy passenger engines - quite good even with certain inherent problems.

Class 461. 2/N & 461. One of the best goods engines on the system, very powerful and reliable, with low axle load. Unfortu-nately only two of class. (No 461 is currently operated by the Railway Preservation Society of Ireland.)

Classes 90 & 100. 2/90. Kept specially for small, very low axle load branches in Cork District, useless for anything else.

Class 279. 1/S. Completely obsolete.

Class 299. 1/299. Completely obsolete.

Class 495. 1/495. Bought from a Brewery for special purposes of shunting Albert Quay, Cork, for which it is especially suited, but not often required.

Class 850. 1/850. Built 1928 for D&SE section, only one of class. Quite powerful, but needs altogether excessive repair but is not replaceable at present.

Class 448. 1/448. A D&SE edition of Standard Goods. Quite good but only one of class.

Jumbo. 1/?. Saddleback tank engine which shunts quays in Waterford.

St. Molaga. 1/?. Light axle load engine confined chiefly to Courtmacsherry Branch.

Sambo. 1/?. No comments.

Argadeen. 1/?. No comments.

A short interim report dated 1st November 1928 was submitted giving the following information:

(a) Particulars of Boilers over 25 years of age.
(b) Boilers available for replacement.
(c) Summary of boiler position on the basis of a 25 years' life.
(d) Summary of boiler position on the basis of a 20 years' life.

A full report is now submitted embracing all the boilers in the Company's possession available for broad gauge locomotives.

NARROW GAUGE LOCOMOTIVES

As the boilers of narrow gauge locomotives and also the vertical boilers of the Sentinel locomotives and coaches are not dealt with herein, it should be stated in passing that the Company's Stock of 36 narrow gauge locomotives are fitted with 18 different classes of boilers. These boilers for some time to come must be dealt with as part of the locomotives in which they are fitted and not as separate units. Where the number of boilers in each class is so small, spare boilers for these 18 classes are out of the question.

The solution of the trouble is in standardisation, but the standardisation of broad gauge types is more important than, and should be proceeded with before the narrow gauge stock is standardised.

BROAD GAUGE LOCOMOTIVES

Boilers of broad gauge locomotives (excluding 2 small Sentinel engines).

The 612 boilers which are available for broad gauge locomotives comprise 63 different types and are fitted into 90 different classes of engines.

Total No	No of Spares	Total No	% of Additional Boilers to Engines	% of Additional Boilers to Total Boilers
502	110	612	21.9%	18%

Statement "A" shows the distribution of the various boiler types among the locomotive classes.

Attention is drawn to the wide variation in the percentage of additional boilers provided for different classes which shows a lack of discrimination and foresight in the arrangement of boiler building programmes in the past.

STANDARDISATION

A close study of Statement "A" shows also that a reasonable provision of spare boilers for the classes of engines to be retained can be dovetailed into a sound scheme of standardisation of locomotive types. For example, as far as the urgent requirements of types already selected for standardisation would allow, renewal programmes should provide for the gradual elimination of those engine classes which contain only (say) 4 engines or less by renewing them as required to pre-arranged standards. In this manner the total number of engine classes now standing at 90 could be reduced to 43 by the renewal of 77 engines, thus dispensing with, and rendering obsolete 48 different classes of engines. In other words by standardising only 15% of the stock no less than 52% of the varying classes would be removed.

RELATION OF BOILER AGE TO MILEAGE

The previous brief report referred to above was based on a 25 years' boiler life, but it was shown that although this basis is satisfactory for the purpose of estimating the arrears of renewals, it is essential that the actual boilers to be renewed should be selected on a service or mileage basis.

The boilers of main line passenger engines might easily reach their ultimate mileage life in 16 or 18 years whereas the boilers of shunting engines would probably attain to twice that age in years before the same ultimate mileage life was reached.

ECONOMIC MILEAGE LIFE OF BOILERS

The next step in the examination of the boiler position is to ascertain what is the economic life of a locomotive boiler under the particular conditions existing on the Great Southern Railways.

In other words, to fix that point in the existence of the boiler beyond which repairs become excessively costly and before which renewal would be premature and wasteful and would sacrifice the asset of further economic usefulness.

Careful consideration has been given to all the material factors which enter into the problem, such as total annual mileage worked by all the Company's stock, average mileage per engine in stock and per engine in use, the mileage worked by individual engines of each class, the quality of the work performed in relation to train loads, the nature of the coal burnt and the effect on steel plates of the water used for generation of steam.

The net result of all the above conditions examined in the light of long engineering and technical experience has led to the decision that boiler maintenance and renewal will be well and adequately provided for and yet not overdone, if a boiler life of 550,000 miles is adopted as a standard governing future practice, and all boilers listed for scrapping after that mileage has been worked.

The average boiler life in years is a figure of little practical value when dealing with the renewal of individual boilers, but it may be mentioned that an actual life of 550,000 miles for each individual boiler corresponds with an average life of 23 years for the whole group.

PRESENT BOILER POSITION

Having fixed the standard life of boilers at 550,000 miles it is now possible to ascertain:

(a) Arrears of boiler renewals to date.
(b) How far arrears can be cancelled by using boilers at present in stock and entered in "Works in Progress" account.
(c) The number of additional boilers to be built or purchased to cancel balance of arrears.
(d) Number of boilers to be renewed annually to maintain normal position.
(e) Spare boilers remaining on stock after cancellation of Arrears of Renewal and additional spare boilers required.

ARREARS OF BOILER RENEWALS

Statement "B" shows that on the basis adopted 94 boilers are overdue for renewal and that 56 of these can be replaced from the Company's stock of new and repaired boilers, leaving an additional 38 new boilers to be built or purchased in order to completely remove arrears of renewals. It will be realised that the 94 boilers which are overdue for scrapping are being maintained at very heavy and uneconomical cost.

The total estimated cost of replacing the 94 boilers overdue for scrapping is:

56 new boilers from Company's stock	£32,081
38 new boilers, say, at £800 each	£30,400
	£62,481

It will be seen therefore that in order to overtake arrears of boiler renewals, and thus eliminate wasteful expenditure on uneconomic boiler repairs, the following action is necessary, and it is recommended that the cost involved should be spread over four years and charged to Reserve as deferred maintenance.

In addition to normal renewals, 56 boilers to be used from stock and 38 additional new boilers provided.

Total cost of 94 boilers (as above), £62,480, or £15,620 per year for four years.

This additional work should be proceeded with as rapidly as practicable under existing conditions subject to the limitation that the yearly cost of such additional work should not exceed £15,620.

Only half of the above expenditure is cash outlay, the other half being represented by boilers withdrawn from existing stock.

NORMAL ANNUAL RENEWAL PROGRAMME

To maintain the standard decided upon (based on a life of 550,000 miles) 22 new boilers will be required annually divided between new boilers in completely new engines and new boilers fitted to repaired engines.

Appendix B

The following table shows the number of boilers renewed each year since Amalgamation of Railways in the Free State:

Total number of new Boilers fitted to Company's Engines

Year	In new engines	Repaired engines	Total
1925	8	8	16
1926	6	17	23
1927	3	12	15
1928	4	13	17

Statement "D" sets out the number of spare boilers of various classes available after 56 boilers have been withdrawn from stock to replace worn-out boilers.

It will be noted that there is a surplus of spare boilers in some classes and these will be used to replace worn-out boilers in the future or scrapped if obsolete or not required.

Reference has been made to the number of engine classes containing only four engines or less.

It is not proposed to sink further capital in providing spare boilers in such cases, which account for 48 different classes containing 77 engines.

Spare boilers are recommended for the remaining broad-gauge engines numbering 502-77 =425, on the basis of 1 spare for every 10 engines or less down to 5.

As shown by Statement "D" there is a shortage of 28 spare boilers on this basis. It is recommended that these be provided, as when available they will greatly accelerate the progress of engines through the Shops. If a spare boiler were ready for immediate use for each locomotive arriving in shops for general repairs, the elimination of the long and costly delay caused by engines having to wait long periods (often upwards of three months) for their own individual boilers would be secured. Thus the working stock could be maintained without having the excessive number of engines always under or awaiting repairs which now appears on our periodical returns.

It is important to note that as the engines actually in use provide fully for present traffic requirements, any permanent reduction in the number of engines constantly under repairs (made possible by the provision of spare boilers) would at once resolve itself into a reduction of the locomotive stock and a consequent saving in maintenance.

Referring again to Statement "D" and omitting classes containing less than five engines, it is shown that 47 spare boilers are required.

Although there are 54 spare boilers on hand, 35 are surplus (that is, over-provision in certain classes) and only 19 are available to meet the required 47 spares, leaving a shortage of 28 spare boilers. It is recommended that these be provided as soon as possible. Of the 35 surplus boilers, 21 will eventually be absorbed as replacements, the remaining 14 should be scrapped.

19th March 1929

N.B. The various statements referred to in the report are voluminous and largely comprised of rather tedious figures. In view of this, they have been omitted.

Extract from CIE Working Timetable for 1946

Time Allowed at Stations for Locomotive Purposes

TRAIN	Athy	Carlow	Kilkenny	Ballymore	
	Mins	Mins	Mins	Mins	Mins
10.30 pm ex K'bridge	40		40	20	
6.40 pm ex W'rford	40		40	20	
4.20 am ex Kildare		40			
5.30 am ex Kilkenny		40			
1.00 pm ex Maryboro'			40	20	
11.45 am ex W'rford			40	20	

TRAIN		Clara			
	Mins	Mins	Mins	Mins	Mins
2.00 am ex K'bridge		40			
2.30 pm ex Athlone		40			

TRAIN		Limer'k Jctn		Clonmel	
	Mins	Mins	Mins	Mins	Mins
2.45 ex Limerick		40		40	
7.15 am ex Limerick		40		40	
11.45 pm ex W'rford		40		40	
7.20 am ex Waterford		40		40	

TRAIN	Ennis	Athenry	Tuam	Claremorris	Tubbercurry
	Mins	Mins	Mins	Mins	Mins
3.40 am ex Limerick	40	40			
12.30 pm ex Tuam				40	40
10.0 am ex Limerick	40	40			
7.45 am ex Tuam	40	40			
7.30 am ex Sligo	40		40	40	40

TRAIN	Enfield	Mullingar	Athlone	Athenry	B'sloe
	Mins	Mins	Mins	Mins	Mins
5.00 am ex Nth Wall	40	40			
9.45 pm ex Nth Wall	40	40			
10.45 pm ex Nth Wall	40	40			
12.00 mn ex Nth Wall	40	40	40		40
8.30 am ex Athlone		40			
8.30 pm ex Galway		40	40	40	
7.15 pm ex Sligo		30			
4.0 pm ex Westport		40			

TRAIN	Bray	Wooden Bridge	Arklow		
	Mins	Mins	Mins	Mins	Mins
8.15 pm ex Nth Wall	30	40			
9.00 pm ex Wexford		40			
7.00 am ex E'corthy		40		40	
3.30 am ex Nth Wall		15		40	

TRAIN	N'castle West		Listowel
	Mins	Mins	Mins
7.15 am ex Limerick	40		40
8.30 am ex Tralee	40		40

TRAIN	Lismore		Dung'van
	Mins	Mins	Mins
4.20 am ex Mallow	40		40
4.10 pm ex Mallow	40		40
4.30 am ex W'rford	40		40
8.45 am ex W'rford	40		40

TRAIN		Duncormick	
	Mins	Mins	Mins
7.00 am ex W'rford		40	
12 noon ex Wexford		40	

TRAIN		Killarney	
	Mins	Mins	Mins
2.30 am ex Mallow		30	
7.45 am ex Mallow		40	
11.0 am ex Tralee		40	

TRAIN	Killorglin	Glenbeigh	
	Mins	Mins	Mins
5.00 am ex Tralee	20	20	
1.45 pm ex Valentia	20		

TRAIN	Dromod	Boyle	
	Mins	Mins	Mins
10.45 pm ex Nth Wall	40	40	
5.30 am ex Mullingar	40		
4.30 pm ex Boyle	40		
7.15 pm ex Sligo	40	40	

TRAIN	Ballmore	Claremorris	
	Mins	Mins	Mins
5.30 am ex Athlone	40	40	
7.00 am ex Athlone	40		
5.45 pm ex Ballina	40		
4.00 pm ex Westport	40	40	

TRAIN		New Ross	
	Mins	Mins	Mins
5.00 ex Wexford		30	
5.20 pm ex W'rford		30	

Appendix C

Drivers of special freight trains will also be allowed time for cleaning at the appointed cleaning places, but the time must not exceed that for the schedule trains.

Time allowed at Stations for Locomotive Purposes

Goods Trains set out below are allowed times at Stations as shown for Fire cleaning purposes

Train	Sallins	Kildare	Portarlington	Ballybrophy	Limerick Jctn	Kilmallock	Charleville	Mallow
	Mins	Mins	Mins	Mins	Mins	Mins	Mins	Mins
12.45 am ex Kingsbridge	40			40				
2.00 am ex Kingsbridge	40		40					
8.00 am ex Thurles					40	40		40
11.30 am ex Kildare					40			
4.00 pm ex Kingsbridge		40		40	40			40
8.45 pm ex Kingsbridge	40			40	40			40
9.45 pm ex Kingsbridge	40			40	40			
10.30 pm ex Kingsbridge	40							
11.45 pm ex Kingsbridge		40		40				
10.30 pm ex Limerick							40	40
12.30 am ex Cork							40	40
2.15 am ex Cork					40	40		40
8.00 am ex Limerick Jctn		40		40				
1.30 pm ex Mallow					40			
2.30 am ex Athlone			40					
4.30 pm ex Thurles			40					
5.10 pm ex Cork								40
12.45 am ex Limerick				40	40			
10.30 pm ex Cork				40	40			40
11.00 pm ex Nenagh			40	40				

Appendix D

List of Irish Locomotives Converted to Burn Oil

Date of conversion	Numbers
Jan 1892	T&DR 5
Sep 1896	B&NCR 51 [Holden system]
June 1903	GS&WR 306 [Holden system]
Mar 1912	MGWR 10
Mar 1936	GNR(I) 172 [B] [C]
May 1945	264 [A]
Sep 1946	GNR(I) 115 [B]
Nov 1946	GNR(I) 2 [B]
Dec 1946	GNR(I) 1 [B], 116 [B]
Jan 1947	330, 378, 390
Mar 1947	373, 379, 388, 393, 396, 398, 630, 638, 639, 643
Apr 1947	249, 346 [D], 352, 354, 376, 386, 391, 394, 395, 409, 500, 624,631, 633, NCC 100 [E]
May 1947	261, 387, 401
June 1947	629
July 1947	255, 259, 263, 334, 340, 344, 351, 356, 501, 583, 625, 626, 636, 641, 642
Aug 1947	118, 140, 182, 338, 587, 607
Sep 1947	153, 252, 260, GNR(I) 159 [B]
Oct 1947	102, 107, 185 [B], 256, 374, 389, 407, 576, 598, 628, NCC 101
Nov 1947	258, 377, 403, 601
Dec 1947	166, 198, 262, 361, 382, 597, 606
1947 [F]	160, 257, 375, 632, 637
Jan 1948	138, 149, 171, 360, 397, 595, 640
Feb 1948	148, 335, 381, 385
Mar 1948	502
1954 [F]	197 [B]

Notes:

GNR(I) = Great Northern Railway (Ireland)
B&NCR = Belfast & Northern Counties Railway
GS&WR = Great Southern & Western Railway
MGWR = Midland Great Western Railway
NCC = Northern Counties Committee
T&DR = Tralee & Dingle Railway (narrow gauge)

All other locomotives listed belonged to GSR/CIE

[A] Cylindrical oil tanks
[B] Laidlaw-Drew burner
[C] Re-converted to coal in December 1936 and back to oil again in October 1945
[D] Sent to GNR(I) for trials in July 1947
[E] Grove burners
[F] Month unknown

Statement of Engine Mileage, Fuel Consumed and Fuel Costs for Year Ended 31st December 1947

Oil-burning Locomotives		
Engine Mileage	1,360,527	
	Gallons	**Gallons per Mile**
Oil Consumed	7,230,792	5.31
	£	**Pence per Mile**
Cost	241,975	42.68
Other Locomotives		
Engine Mileage	6,387,087	
	Tons	**Lbs per Mile**
Fuel consumed (coal and turf)	233,461	81.88
	£	**Pence per Mile**
	1,027,907	38.62
Average Cost per Ton		
Coal Fuel	88s 1.35d	
Other Fuels	36s 6.22d	

Appendix F

Details of Run to Cork of Oil-burning Locomotive No 185 on 20th February 1948
Mixed Special Load 56=45

Station	Arrive	Depart	Steam pressure	Water	Remarks
Kingsbridge		10.19	150	Full	
Clondalkin	10.39		150	Full	Passed
Sallins	11.20	11.26	145	¾	Took water
Kildare	12.12	13.00	150	Full	Repairs to gland spindle
Portarlington	13.35	13.40	145	Full	Took water
Maryborough	14.13		145	¾	Passed
Ballybrophy	15.04	15.10	150	Full	Took water
Thurles	15.55		145	¾	Passed
Limerick Jnct	16.55	17.05	140	Full	Water. Burner examined
Kilmallock	18.00	18.45	150	Full	45 wagons off, 11 left
Charleville	18.55		150	Full	Passed
Mallow	19.05	19.25	150	Full	2 wagons off, 9 left
Rathpeacon	20.30	20.40	150	Full	Blocked by signals
Kilbarry	20:55	20:58	140	Full	Blocked by signals
Cork	21.00		140	Full	

Total time taken: 10 hours 41 minutes.
Total time stopped: 2 hours 33 minutes.
Actual running time: 8 hours 8 minutes.

Oil Consumption.
The tender had 1,300 gallons on starting and 610 gallons on arrival in Cork, that is, 690 gallons were consumed on the trip, of which 56 gallons were consumed during standing time and 634 gallons in actual running. This equates to 3.83 gallons per mile, or 4.1 total.

Appendix G

Test Run of No 356 to Cork on 9th June 1953

Station	Arrive	Depart	Gain*	Loss*	Remarks
Kingsbridge	-	10.48			
Sallins	11.33	11.40	12	-	Water stop
Monasterevan	12.42	12.47	6	-	Signals
Portarlington	13.00	13.18	5	-	Water/signals
Ballybrophy	14.29	15.45	10	-	Up/down enterprises crossed
Thurles	16.33	16.45	4	-	Water
Knocklong	18.10	18.27	-	5	Heavy rain and poor visibility
Kilmallock	18.47	18.58	3	-	Weather improved
Mallow	20.10	20.34	-	8	Delay awaiting fresh crew
Blarney	21.40	21.41	-	11	Signal check, poor steaming
Rathpeacon	21.58	22.03	2	-	Signal check
Cork	22.29	-	18		

* Gain or loss on Goods Sectional Running Times as per Working Timetable.

Appendix H

Runs by CC1 23rd July to 17th October 1957

Date	Destination	Miles [1]	Miles [2]	Remarks
23-7-57	-	-	-	First steaming. TIA blow-down valve became stuck open with swarf from boiler.
30-7-57	-	-	-	Second steaming.
4-8-57	-	-	-	Third steaming. Brake problems.
6-8-57	Inchicore Yard	1½	1½	Moved for first time under own power, 25mph achieved.
7-8-57	Inchicore Yard	½	2	Collision with No 1100.
8-8-57	Inchicore Yard	4	6	Handled well, 30mph. Inspected by M. Armand of SNCF.
13-8-57	Sallins	36	42	CME on board. Loco behaved well.
14-8-57	Kildare	60	102	Light engine, 57mph. Poor steaming.
15-8-57	Inchicore Yard	5	107	Load trials=22 with ease up 1 in 100 gradient. Lineside fires.
16-8-57	Newbridge	49	156	Carriage roof on fire at Newbridge. 63mph on return.
17-8-57	Works	-	-	Seat welded under No 2 end.
19-8-57	Clondalkin	7	163	Observer rode below locomotive.
20-8-57	Portarlington	81	244	Light engine, 63mph. Excessive oil consumption.
21-8-57	Inchicore Yard	5	249	Load=22. CIE Chairman and BnM officials.
22-8-57	Kildare	58	307	-
23-8-57	Sallins/Kildare	91	398	-
26-8-57	Newbridge	49	447	Demonstration run for benefit of Union Officials.
27-8-57	Kildare	58	505	Modified firebars, better steaming.
28-8-57	Sallins	36	541	Load=7. Carriage roof fires.
29-8-57	Sallins (2 runs)	72	613	-
31-8-57	Works	-	-	2 brick arches fitted to reduce sparks. Boiler washed out and found to be very dirty.
2-9-57	Kildare	60	673	Fewer sparks. Oil consumption heavy.
3-9-57	Kildare	60	733	Load=7.
4-9-57	Kildare	60	793	Load=11. Better steaming. Reached Kildare in 42 minutes without carriage fires.
5-9-57	Kildare	60	853	Load=15.
6-9-57	Kildare	60	913	Load=17. C.S. Cocks on board.
7-9-57	Works	-	-	Rocking grate fitted. In Works until 21st Sep. Engine inspected and rapid wear found in valve driving gears. Chain case modified where chain had made contact. Bogie bearers 'scored'.
23-9-57	Lucan	12	925	-
24-9-57	Sallins	35	960	70 mph. Light engine. Axleboxes less warm.
25-9-57	Cork	166	1126	Light engine. Heavy oil consumption. Replenishment of oil from sumps became leading pre-occupation.
26-9-57	From Cork	166	1292	As above.
27-9-57	Sallins	35	1327	Load=11. Excessive oil consumption especially past crossheads.
2-10-57	Mullingar	122	1449	Light engine. Lively riding on curves.
4-10-57	Cork	166	1615	Load=11. Reduced oil consumption but still needed refilling at stops. Steaming best ever.

Date	Destination	Miles [1]	Miles [2]	Remarks
Continued:				
5-10-57	From Cork	169	1784	Refused to reverse at Inchicore. Steaming better than ever, high speed finish to run. Train continued to Island Bridge and reversed there.
8-10-57	Portarlington	82	1866	Centre firebars could not be kept covered.
9-10-57	Sallins	33	1899	Light engine to try smoke deflectors at one end. Great improvement.
10-10-57	Portarlington	82	1981	Load=6. Mr. Dudley on footplate.
11-10-57	Sallins (2 runs)	66	2047	Smoke lifting good when observed from lineside.
12-10-57	Kildare	60	2107	Light engine. Two hot boxes on No 1 bogie on return trip.
16-10-57	Hazlehatch/Straffan	40	2147	Broken rings removed from cylinder cocks.
17-10-57	Works	-	-	Locomotive lifted.

[1] Miles run on day   [2] Accumulated mileage

Appendix I

Runs by CC1 to Kildare September 1957

Three runs made from Inchicore to Kildare, with increasingly heavy loads, on the 4th, 5th and 6th September 1957, demonstrated quite conclusively the limiting evaporation possible with the locomotive in the condition it then was. On each run the total evaporation rate was constant at between 13,000 and 14,000 lbs/hr. As loading increased, so did the time to do the 28½ miles:

Date	Load	Tons	Time
4th September	5 bogies + 1 van	160	42 minutes
5th September	7 bogies + 1 van	225	49 minutes
6th September	8 bogies + 1 van	255	55 minutes

Similar conditions applied throughout each run as follows:

Smokebox vacuum	2 in (100-110psi turbine pressure needed)
Smokebox temperature	820°F
Duct entry temperature	660°F
Fan exit temperature	500°F (extrapolated from result of stationary test)
Feed water temperature	190°F

Turf consumption was accurately measured on the last two days (including lighting up from 100psi, the return trip to Kildare, and putting away at the completion of the day's work). On 5th September 2.18 tons were consumed and on 6th September 2.56 tons. This represents rates of 84 and 99lbs/train mile respectively.

On 6th September, the return run from Kildare was made with the 255 ton train at an average speed of 47½mph from start to stop.

The point to notice is that the locomotive can produce its maximum evaporation at all speeds, if necessary, and with or without the regulator being open.

Appendix J

Trial Run of CC1 to Cork 4th October 1957 – Load 5 Bogie Carriages and 1 Heating Van = 165 Tons

Place	Time	Mile post	Boiler pressure	Steam chest pressure	Cut-off %	Temperature °F			Vacuum		Turbine Pressure	Feed water °F		Water gauge level
						Smoke box	Duct	Steam	Smokebox	Duct		Pump	Clack	
Inchicore dep	10.57.08		235											
	10.58.45	2	210	128	50	740	625	502	1¾		100	80	190	⅞
	11.02.31	3	190	120	40	776	640	508	1½	3	100	81	210	½
	11.05.25	4	180	110	38	792	650	520	1 5/8	3 3/8	105	81	194	¼
	11.09.46	6	197	120	30	838	670	530	1 7/8	3 5/8	115	80	172	⅓
	11.13.07	8	210	125	28	830	670	530	1 7/8		112	78	180	⅓
	11.16.06	10	210	110	28	818	670	520	2 1/16		113		180	½
	11.21.26	14	198	110	28	778	645	515	2	3 7/8	115	80	168	⅓
	11.27.20	18	198	110	28	829	684	540	2 1/16	4	130	82	174	¼
	11.34.05	23	212	140	20	800	660		2		115	82	161	½
	11.39.29	27	180	110	25	810	650	475	1 7/8		118		178	⅛
Kildare arr	11.43.58		200											¼
Kildare dep	11.50.43	30	222											Full
	11.56.40	34	190	110	22	800	660	530	2 1/16		115	85	152	Full
	12.00.45	38	195	110	22	795	660	530	2 1/16	3 7/8	115			Full
Portarlington	12.05.40			·										⅞
Portarlington	12.14.35		240											
	12.20.05	44	230	160	22	805	650	510	2		115	90	165	Full
	12.27.24	49	208	120	35	800	653	495	2					⅞
	12.31.35	52	206	120	25	785	640	503	2	3¼	115	86	170	¾
	12.37.07	56	214	90	25	800	670	520	2		115	84	160	Full
	12.43.54	62	207	90	38	760	625	485	2		120	85	188	¾
	12.49.28	66	218											⅞
Ballybrophy	12.51.00													⅞
Ballybrophy	12.55.36		212											Full
	12.59.02	68	222	120	25	790	655	520	1 7/8	3½	105	91	196	⅞
	13.04.28	72	225											
	13.10.48	77	246	60	25	773	630	520	1 1/16		57	88	174	Full
	13.16.04	81	230	125	38	710			1½					
	13.20.28	84	240	150	25	705	600	485	¾		70	90	188	Full
Thurles	13.24.33													¾
Thurles	13.42.45		250											Full
	13.50.35	90	250	50	25	760								Full
	13.55.45	94	207	110	25	768	650	502	1¾		100	88	160	Full
	14.00.58	98	226	120	25	815	655	515	2		112	88	190	Full
	14.05.50	102	210	110	25	796	660	520	1 7/8		110	88	170	¾
	14.10.32	106	200											
	14.13.13	108	210	120	38	808	660	500	2	3 7/8	112	89	174	Full
	14.18.50	112	190		50									
	14.21.40	114	200	100	25	786	652	500	2	3½	100	91	180	¾
	14.26.31	118	213	120	25	759	630	488	1 9/16		92			⅝
	14.31.07	122	198	108	25	790	633	490			86	95	160	½

Appendix J

Place	Time	Mile post	Boiler pressure	Steam chest pressure	Cut-off %	Temperature °F			Vacuum		Turbine Pressure	Feed water °F		Water gauge level
						Smokebox	Duct	Steam	Smokebox	Duct		Pump	Clack	
Kilmallock	14.34.08		220											⅝
Kilmallock	14.39.55		235	128	40									Full
	14.48.00	128	210	135	30	752	618	490	1 13/16		105	100	176	Full
	14.51.42	130	200											
	14.57.27	134	205	100	25	785	640	510			112			
	15.01.50	138	202	110	25	748	630	500			118	96	186	Full
	15.07.22	142	198		50	672	573		1		75			Full
Mallow	15.10.58													Full
Mallow	15.26.20		245											Full
	15.30.30	146	204	110	45	732	600	485	1½		95			Full
	15.40.03	150	185	110	45	718	620	496	2		120	106	190	⅞
	15.44.51	152	188	105	35	770	620	500	1 5/16		67	100	180	½
	15.55.25	160	190		50									
Cork	16.07.00													Full

Notes: Signal checks at MPs 66 and 112. PWS 25mph at MP77. Top of banks MPs 138 and 150.

Appendix K

Trial Run of CC1 from Cork 5th October 1957 — Load 5 Bogie Carriages and 1 Heating Van = 165 tons

Place	Time	Mile post	Boiler pressure	Steam chest pressure	Cut-off %	Temperature °F			Vacuum		Turbine Pressure	Feed water °F		Water gauge level
						Smokebox	Duct	Steam	Smokebox	Duct		Pump	Clack	
Cork	09.55.36		235											Full
	10.02.26		160											
	10.09.30	163	182	175	50	710	635	480	1¾		115			Full
	10.15.26	162	178	171	50	740	640	485	1 5/8		113			⅞
	10.18.08	161	195	70	25	745	650	490			115			Full
	10.20.22	160	200	80	25	708			1¾					
	10.22.40	159	213	90	25	712			1 5/8					Full
	10.24.44	158	220	84	25	708			1½					Full
	10.26.37	157	220	170	25	748			1 9/16					
	10.30.18	155	200	140	25	690			1 7/16					⅝
	10.32.12	154	200	140	25	715								¼
	10.36.49	152	200	100	25	718			1½					½
	10.38.42	150	210		50	675			3/8					⅛
Mallow	10.45.00		220											¾
Mallow	11.00.25		245											Full
	11.02.37	144	212	180	35	665	590	450	1 3/8		100	Cold	194	⅞
	11.07.17	142	183	130	35	710	610	460	1 5/16				150	⅓
	11.11.53	140	188	80	25	735	640	495	1½					¼
	11.17.25	136	210	65	25	735	635	513	1 7/16		95			½
	11.22.28	132	202	87	25	750	650	500	1½		95			⅝

Place	Time	Mile post	Boiler pressure	Steam chest pressure	Cut-off %	Temperature °F			Vacuum		Turbine Pressure	Feed water °F		Water gauge level
						Smokebox	Duct	Steam	Smokebox	Duct		Pump	Clack	
	11.27.43	128	200	65	25	715	640	510	1 9/16					
Kilmallock	11.32.38		240											¾
Kilmallock	11.41.38		245											Full
	11.45.43	123	248	125	25						70			Full
	11.48.07	122	212	125	25									Full
	11.51.43	120	212	110	25									Full
	11.56.47	116	190	105	25									7/8
	12.01.31	112	180	100	25									¾
	12.06.17	108	200		50									½
	12.11.02	104	210	110	25									Full
	12.15.58	100	210	100	25									7/8
	12.20.22	96												
Goolds Cross	12.21.45		250											Full
Goolds Cross	12.24.15		250											
	12.28.21	93	225	125	30						75			Full
Thurles	12.37.30		240											7/8
Thurles	12.53.50		248											Full
	13.05.35	80	190	70	25	690	600	490			93		140	¾
	13.11.00	76	180	65	30	707	625	495	1½		112		143	5/8
	13.17.55	71	180	60	30	700								½
	13.19.10	70	180	60	30	720	625	500	1½		100			½
	13.23.59	66	172	80	30	700	620	485	1½		100		160	½
	13.28.29	62	229		50	726	650		1 5/8		100			Full
	13.33.54	58	218	85	20	765	670	485	1½		103		140	Full
	13.41.07	52	200	80	20	724			1 9/16					Full
	13.45.12	48	220	80	20	760	660	485			105		150	Full
Portarlington	13.52.14		245											Full
Portarlington	14.02.40		250											Full
	14.06.58	40	203	70	25	650	570	460	1		55		190	Full
	14.11.58	36	200	70	25	748	650	500	1 9/16		100		150	7/8
	14.17.04	32	180	85	25	713	630	490	1½		110			5/8
	14.23.00	28	180	65	25	748	653	483	1½		90		144	¼
	14.27.43	24	203	70	25	738	650	480	1½		100		142	½
	14.32.08	20	211	80	20	760	670	484	1 5/8		105		142	¾
	14.36.23	16	207	70	20	750	670	485			105		136	¾
	14.40.21	12	220	80	20	770	670	484			106		144	Full
	14.44.30	8	225	80	20	750	652	483			103		144	Full
	14.48.39	4	230		50	740								Full
	14.50.28	2	245		50									Full
Inchicore	14.52.00		248											Full

Note: Stopped at Goold's Cross due to ballast train not cleared section, Regulator closed 1 ½ minutes before Newbridge.

CIE STEAM LOCOMOTIVES

Class	Wheels	Cylinders	Driving Wheels	Boiler Pressure	Tractive Effort	Weight
C2/455	4-4-2T	18in x 26in	6ft 0in	160	15,912	64-16
D2/321	4-4-0	18in x 26in	6ft 7in	180	16,315	55-06
D4/333	4-4-0	18in x 26in	5ft 8½in	180	18,800	51-10
J4/257	0-6-0	19in x 26in	5ft 1¾in	160	20,670	46-11
J5/623	0-6-0	19in x 26in	5ft 8in	175	20,530	47-11
J15/101	0-6-0	18in x 24in	5ft 1¾in	160	17,170	37-13
J18/593	0-6-0	18in x 24in	5ft 3in	150	15,737	38-10
K1/372	2-6-0	19in x 28in	5ft 6in	180	23,432	62-04
K3/355	2-6-0	19in x 26in	5ft 1¾in	160	20,672	57-02
CC1	0-6-6-0	12in x 14in (4)	3ft 7in	250	20,000	118-00

CIE DIESEL LOCOMOTIVES

Class	Wheels	Builder	Horse Power	Weight
A	Co-Co	Metrovick	1200	84-12
B/1100	Bo-Bo	CIE Inchicore	915	75-00
B/121	Bo-Bo	GM	950	61-00
C	Bo-Bo	Metrovick	550	58-00

GNR(I) STEAM LOCOMOTIVES

Class	Wheels	Cylinders	Driving Wheels	Boiler Pressure	Tractive Effort	Weight
QL	4-4-0	17¾in x 26in	6ft 7in	175	15,424	49-10
QLs*	4-4-0	18½in x 26in	6ft 7in	175	16,755	49-19
S2	4-4-0	19in x 26in	6ft 7in	175	17,673	52-02
T2	4-4-2T	18in x 24in	5ft 9in	175	16,763	65-15

* Superheated version of the QL class.

SR/BR STEAM LOCOMOTIVES

Class	Wheels	Cylinders	Driving Wheels	Boiler Pressure	Tractive Effort	Weight
H1	4-4-2	19in x 26in	6ft 7½in	200	20,070	68-05
M7	0-4-4T	18½in x 26in	5ft 7in	175	19,755	60-04
MN	4-6-2	18in x 24in (3)	6ft 2in	280	37,515	94-15
Q1	0-6-0	19in x 26in	5ft 1in	230	30,080	89-05
Leader	0-6-6-0	12¼in x 15in (6)	5ft 1in	280	26,350	131-00

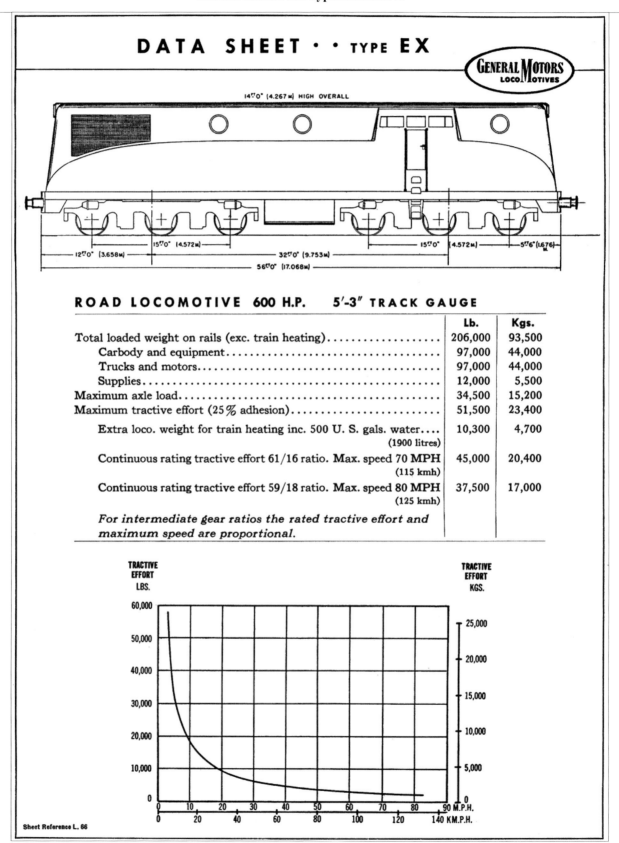

DATA SHEET ·· TYPE EX

General Motors LOCOMOTIVES

14'0" (4.267 M) HIGH OVERALL

15'0" (4.572 M) 15'0" (4.572 M) 5'6" (1.676 M)
12'0" (3.658 M) 32'0" (9.753 M)
56'0" (17.068 M)

ROAD LOCOMOTIVE 600 H.P.   5'-3" TRACK GAUGE

	Lb.	Kgs.
Total loaded weight on rails (exc. train heating)..................	206,000	93,500
Carbody and equipment.....................................	97,000	44,000
Trucks and motors..	97,000	44,000
Supplies..	12,000	5,500
Maximum axle load..	34,500	15,200
Maximum tractive effort (25% adhesion).......................	51,500	23,400
Extra loco. weight for train heating inc. 500 U. S. gals. water.... (1900 litres)	10,300	4,700
Continuous rating tractive effort 61/16 ratio. Max. speed 70 MPH (115 kmh)	45,000	20,400
Continuous rating tractive effort 59/18 ratio. Max. speed 80 MPH (125 kmh)	37,500	17,000

For intermediate gear ratios the rated tractive effort and maximum speed are proportional.

TRACTIVE EFFORT LBS.   TRACTIVE EFFORT KGS.

Sheet Reference L. 66

BULLEID AND THE TURF BURNER

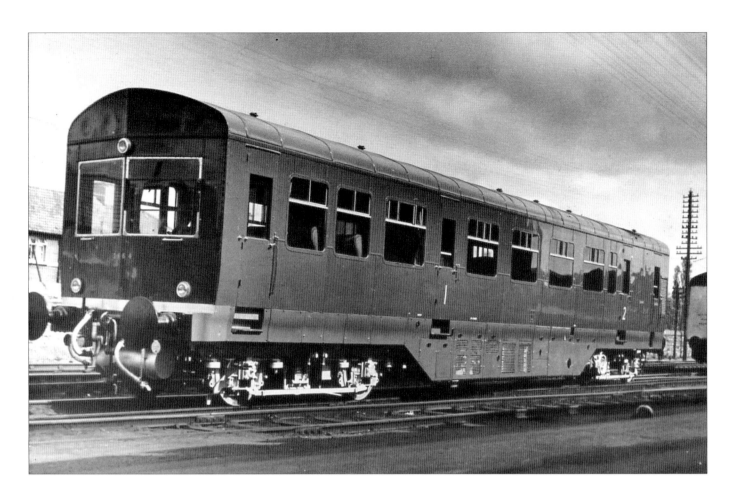

Above:

Despite his belief in a future for steam traction, Bulleid was also astute enough to recognise that alternative motive power was preferable for certain types of traffic. Accordingly, from June 1951 onwards, the first of 60 AEC railcars were delivered; this number was later increased to 66, the final 6 being built at Inchicore using engines and transmissions delivered from Britain. Later still, 4 additional vehicles were constructed, intended for the narrow gauge CIE services.

Overleaf:

The culmination of the idea. CC1 almost in its final form, recorded at Inchicore. By this stage, the engine had received its large smoke deflectors, but was yet to be painted in green. The white wheel below the cab door is the handbrake, which Click commented required a feat of gymnastics, not to be dwelt upon, if applied whilst running.

There would be many stages in design to go through before this, the final form, was eventually arrived at. According to H.A.V. Bulleid in his masterly tome "Bulleid of the Southern", the final drawing for the boiler was shown by Bulleid to R.C. Bond of British Railways, the latter allegedly too surprised to say anything. Bulleid then broke the silence with the remark, "I know what you are thinking, this could only be the work of the late Heath-Robinson". Such a remark was surely an unnecessary criticism of himself.

As a designer, it has been popular to ridicule aspects of Bulleid's work in the past, to do this though is unfair. Here was a designer who was prepared to experiment, someone who, with hindsight, did get it wrong sometimes, but in other areas his successes have been forgotten. Certainly not all the aspects of his various designs were poor. What engineer could be said to have been 100% successful in any area?

Time was the biggest difficulty for Bulleid, his professional life was always dictated by circumstances outside his control. Who then can blame the man for attempting the impossible. Without his efforts the story of the steam engine would be dull by comparison.

(Deegan-photo, copyright CIE)

INDEX